FOR GAZA'S CHILDREN

Black, Brown And Jewish
Writers And Poets Speak Out

FOR GAZA'S CHILDREN

Black, Brown And Jewish Writers And Poets Speak Out

Marc Lamont Hill, Haki R. Madhubuti and Keith Gilyard

Editors

THIRD WORLD PRESS
FOUNDATION
Established 1967

CHICAGO

Third World Press
Publishers since 1967
Chicago

Distributed by Ingram Publisher Services

First Edition
Printed in the United States of America

ISBN: 978-0-88378-437-2

24   23   22   21   87654321

Cover by Donte Neal
Interior layout by Relana Johnson

www.thirdworldpressfoundation.org

Dedication

Edward Said

Noam Chomsky

Mahmoud Darwish

Rashida Tlaib*

Adrienne Rich

Cori Bush*

June Jordan

Jamaal Bowman*

Angela Davis

Norman Finkelstein

Cornel West

Chris Hedges

& always Gwendolyn Brooks

& the Palestinian people

*Rep. Rashida Tlaib is the first and only Palestinian Congresswoman to serve in the United States Congress. Rep. Cori Bush is a Black woman who took her progressive values to Congress and became a part of the "squad" and a powerful voice for the unheard. Rep. Jamaal Bowman also played a vital role in speaking and acting for the poor and marginalized. Rep. Bowman and Rep. Bush were recently defeated in their primaries with the aid of pro-Israel lobbying funds with AIPAC (American Israel Public Affairs Committee) putting in millions of dollars.

"This is *precisely* the time when artists go to work. There is no time for despair, no place for self-pity, no need for silence, no room for fear. We speak, we write, we do language. That is how civilizations heal. I know the world is bruised and bleeding, and though it is important not to ignore its pain, it is also critical to refuse to succumb to its malevolence. Like failure, chaos contains information that can lead to knowledge—even wisdom. Like art."

—Toni Morrison

Table of Contents

Introduction

Marc Lamont Hill, Haki R. Madhubuti and Keith Gilyard

For Gaza's Children: Black, Brown and Jewish Writers and Poets Speak Out provides a timely and powerful response to the political, moral, and humanitarian crisis presently taking place in the Gaza Strip. We decided to produce this anthology in the weeks following October 7, 2023. On that tragic day, a Hamas-led attack caused the death of nearly 1,200 Israelis citizens and the capture of numerous Israeli hostages. In response to Hamas' attack, Israel has waged an ongoing and unrelenting assault that has killed more than 23,000 Palestinians, including over 9,000 innocent children, and permanently displaced 1.7 of Gaza's remaining 2.1 million residents. In addition to being morally indefensible, such actions are a flagrant violation of both the spirit and letter of international law, nearly all modern conventions of war, and almost every established human rights standard.

The impact of Israel's assault on Gaza is not limited to the astronomical death toll. Beyond the stunning number of Palestinians who have been killed or injured, Israel's recent bombardment of Gaza has caused the destruction of hospitals, schools, cultural centers, religious sites, and ancient landmarks. Even if the violence in Gaza were to stop immediately, and forever, the current generation of Palestinian children would still be burdened with the impossible task of rescuing their families, communities, traditions, and freedom dreams from the rubble of settler-colonial destruction.

As the violence in Gaza continues, the lives of Palestinian children have been increasingly precarious and vulnerable. With each passing day, even more Gazan children are forced to witness the death of their families, the destruction of their schools, and the erasure of any semblance of normalcy and peace. While much the world remains vocally supportive or silently complicit with Israeli government's actions, Palestinian children are being steadily robbed of the most essential elements of childhood: innocence, imagination, exploration, safety, and play. In nearly every way, Israel's purported war on Gaza has also become a full-fledged war on Palestinian children.

As we develop new moral frameworks, political agendas, and practical strategies to produce justice in Israel and Palestine, these efforts must be shaped by an unwavering commitment to the 1.1 million infants, toddlers, adolescents, and teenagers who live in the region. As we determine the status of our global struggle for liberation---whether progress or victory, regression or defeat---we must use the lives, experiences, and futures of Palestinian children as our primary indicator.

Although the present moment inspires great feelings of pessimism, we remain prisoners of hope. Our hope is not baseless or naïve, but rather deeply rooted in the recognition of our collective progress. Although mainstream media and political institutions have sanitized Israeli violence by framing it as a morally justifiable "War on Hamas," everyday people around the world have rightly recognized the assault on Gaza as a morally unjustifiable war on the Palestinian people. As powerful governments are fiercely protecting the status quo in Israel-Palestine, the citizens of those governments have still risked their freedom and safety to defiantly demand justice. At a moment where critics of Israel are being smeared, demonized, fired, and even criminalized, a growing cadre of courageous freedom fighters has stood in steadfast solidarity with the struggle for Palestinian liberation. Despite powerful white supremacist narratives about an uncivilized Middle East, and compelling capitalist logics that stress the importance of individualism and isolation, people around the world continue to recognize and affirm the fundamental dignity and humanity of all oppressed people around the world.

This sober but radical hope provides the foundation for our book project. We firmly believe that our children are the stewards of our liberation. When we prioritize our children, we are also prioritizing a world shaped by peace, safety, love, and justice. When we protect our children, we are also protecting our most beautiful legacies and coveted traditions. When we invest in our children, we are also investing in our most audacious freedom dreams and our most impossible future worlds. The children of Gaza, and indeed all of Palestine, are no different.

Driven by this commitment, we have decided to assemble an anthology that prioritizes children. We hope to contribute to the present moment of radical resistance and revolutionary possibility by placing the lives, experiences, conditions, feelings, perspectives, and stories of the region's children at the center of our social, cultural, moral, legal, and political analysis.

We view this anthology as an offering of radical solidarity and revolutionary love. We hope that the book will not only deepen our base of knowledge and expand our inventory of ideas, but also inspire readers to stand beside our Palestinian family as they relentlessly struggle for justice. May this text serve as a powerful reminder that our individual and collective freedom requires the liberation of the entire human family.

I

The Denial of Palestinian Childhood
Marc Lamont Hill

In a world of unmerited suffering and unjustified oppression, children provide a vital source of hope. Our children remind us of our grandest possibilities. With the birth of every baby, we are confronted by the power of effortless sacrifice and boundless love. With the development of every infant, we are compelled by the intellectual power of unrestrained imagination and unbridled wonder. With the growth of every adolescent, we are challenged by the transformative power of principled discipline and revolutionary patience. Through the lives of children, we have justified our most audacious hopes and inspired our most ambitious dreams. Our children are the best of us.

The value of children is not limited to intangible aspirations or abstract ideals. In virtually every nation, the political commitment and moral authority of the powerful are revealed within the collective condition of the children. In almost every civilization, the engines of social transformation have been primarily powered by the creative ingenuity of the youth. In nearly every social and political organization, the promise of institutional stability has been directly tied to an investment in young people. In every society, the preservation of valued customs and treasured traditions demands a firm embrace of the next generation. Through the lives of children, we are granted an unflinching assessment of our most impressive successes and most devastating failures.

In the West, the value of children is revealed in our collective understandings of childhood. Our modern religious traditions have defined childhood as a time of moral innocence and spiritual purity. Our intellectual and artistic traditions have painted childhood as a period of unrestrained joy and unbridled imagination. Our legal doctrines have constructed childhood as a time of uncertainty and institutional mercy. In virtually all of our cultural traditions and social institutions, we offer reverence for the sanctity, beauty, power, and possibilities of childhood.

But who gets to be a child?

***

On October 30, 2023, a stunning piece of information was presented to the world. The Euro-Med Human Rights Monitor, an independent youth-led international human rights organization, issued a global press release about the rising death rates of children living in the Gaza Strip. According to the group, 3,457 children had been killed in the

24 days since October 7th, when Israel launched its most recent military attack.

3,457 dead children in 24 days.
144 children per day.
9 children each hour.
1 child every 7 minutes.

Despite this horrific death toll, the world remained silent. Mainstream media outlets provided scant news coverage. Powerful politicians showed little outrage. In the face of indefensible violence, the primary response from the global community was unashamedly cynical, shamelessly reactionary, and shamefully feckless.

Why did the events of October 7th earn tireless mainstream media attention while the revelations of October 30th were virtually ignored? Why would the world weep for Ukraine's recently fallen children while neglecting the young martyrs of Gaza? Why was so much of the international community galvanized by the suspected death of a single innocent Israeli baby yet indifferent to the mass murder of Palestinian children? The answer is sad, but simple.

For much of the world, Gaza has no children. Employing a White-supremacist view of the children of Gaza, we struggle to see the humanity of Palestinian children. We are unable to assess their value. We fail to see their beauty. We are incapable of acknowledging, much less protecting, their innocence. In a world that racializes Palestinians as non-White, the children of Gaza do not elicit the same visceral reaction after death and injury as Israeli children.

But the attack on Gaza's children cannot be measured only in death and injury. It must also be measured in trauma. With every failed ceasefire negotiation, Gaza's children become increasingly susceptible to premature death, sudden attack at any moment, the crippling knowledge that at any moment, they, their parents, their siblings or their friends could be killed. With every passing day, Palestinian children are more thoroughly robbed of their innocence. Childhood is a time of learning. In societies across the world, childhood is viewed as a time for unbridled curiosity and deep discovery. But the children of Gaza have been robbed of that time.

Israeli bombs and artillery have destroyed most of the schools and all the universities—every single one—in Gaza. Playgrounds, parks, and libraries have been destroyed en masse. All the museums in Gaza are gone, as are most of the mosques, sites of learning and socializing.

Palestinian children who survive this moment's unspeakable horror will do so completely cut off from their own past, their own history.

Israel is prosecuting a genocidal war, not just through the practice of daily homicide, but also through its murderous rampage against the past and the future of and for Palestinian children. In robbing Palestinian children of their childhood, they create misery in the present, steal the children's development and education about themselves and their people, and cripple their development for the future.

Israel's genocidal war targets childhood itself. And that genocide is allowed to happen because of the longstanding, White-supremacist tradition of denying Black and Brown people access to childhood, access to childhood as a category, as a practice, right, as an identity. Black and Brown children are not seen as the innocent, budding wonders that White children are, but as small, latent threats who will grow into potentially dangerous adults. They are objects of fear rather than hope. Seeing Palestinian children in that light makes it much easier not only to kill them, but to kill them with impunity.

***

After 5 months of this genocidal war, more children had died in Gaza (12,300) than in every other global conflict combined (12,193) over a four-year (2019-2022) period. By the 9-month mark, the death rates of children in Gaza from violence, hunger, and disease had become the fastest in modern history. Today, the war on Gaza's children has only grown more brutal and vicious.

Those are the appalling statistics we hear every day. As Israel's genocidal rampage through Gaza continues, disease, malnutrition, and lack of water and sanitary facilities are taking more lives in addition to those snuffed out by Israel's American-supplied weapons.

The children of Gaza who do not become mere statistics in those tallies have survived those horrors. Those children, who, for the last ten months, have not been able to learn, have not known safety, have experienced terror and loss beyond imagining, are the victims of this war as well. Yet we don't see those Palestinian children as we do the perceived White children of Israel or of Ukraine. We remain silent about the children of Gaza, whether they have been robbed of their lives or "merely" robbed of their childhoods.

Dare to Accurately Name
the Horror of Gaza: Genocide
Haki R. Madhubuti

"If We Must Die"
Claude McKay*   1889 – 1948

If we must die, let it not be like hogs
Hunted and penned in an inglorious spot,
While round us bark the mad and hungry dogs,
Making their mock at our accursed lot.
If we must die, O let us nobly die,
So that our precious blood not be shed
In vain; then even the monsters we defy
Shall be constrained to honor us though dead!
O kinsmen! we must meet the common foe!
Though far outnumbered let us show us brave,
And for their thousand blows deal one deathblow!
What though before us lies the open grave?
Like men we'll face the murderous, cowardly pack,
Pressed to the wall, dying, but fighting back!

*A major Harlem Renaissance poet who died in the year of the founding
of the state of Israel, or the Palestinian's Nakba ("Catastrophe").

"If I Must Die"
Refaat Alareer*   1979 – 2023

If I must die,
you must live
to tell my story
to sell my things
to buy a piece of cloth
and some strings,
(make it white with a long tail)
so that a child, somewhere in Gaza
while looking heaven in the eye
awaiting his dad who left in a blaze—
and bid no one farewell

7

not even to his flesh
not even to himself—
sees the kite, my kite you made, flying up above
and thinks for a moment an angel is there
bringing back love
If I must die
let it bring hope
let it be a tale.

*This is the final poem by Palestinian poet and academic Refaat Alareer, known as the "voice of Gaza," who was killed in an Israeli strike on December 7, 2023.

Yes, it is often the poets who bring clarity, who warn us, forcing us to think beyond the possibility of one's own life or death. The great poet Claude McKay's people had experienced genocide during the Middle Passage, where shipload after shipload of Europeans disposed into the ocean the bodies of both dead and alive enslaved Africans during their forced voyage to the West (see *Before the Mayflower* by Lerone Bennett Jr., sixth ed., 1984 and *The Destruction of Black Civilization* by Chancellor Williams, 1974). The European trade in African women, men, and, yes, babies numbered in the tens of millions, and now, during a contemporary genocide, the Palestinian poet, the voice of Gaza, Refaat Alareer, a direct descendant of the magnificent unofficial Poet Laureate of Palestine, Mahmoud Darwish, had failed to escape the torrential bombs from the Israeli Defense Force (IDF) in the aftermath of the shocking murders and human violations committed on October 7, 2023, by Hamas, the fighting branch among the 2.3 million Gazan people imprisoned within the 25 x 5-mile open "concentration camp."

Gaza is presently occupied by the state of Israel and remains the largest concentration camp in the world, making the country an apartheid nation-state. As of this writing, the calculated number of deaths in Gaza is 37,700 humans, which includes over 20,000 children. However, the highly respected, prestigious, peer-reviewed British medical journal *The Lancet* has warned that the true death toll in the Gaza genocide could be 186, 000 or more (July 5, 2024). These numbers continue to increase in a "war" of less than eight months, as witnessed by a vigilant international community of students, political activists, human rights workers, and concerned citizens of the world who have collectively defined these horrendous events as genocide. This terror, this disproportionate response on the part of Israel with systematic bombing and destruction of the Gazan population, is now recognized worldwide as a "war" crime. These genocidal actions by Israel have been confirmed by Senator Bernie

Sanders; historians John Mearsheimer and Norman Finkelstein; Ilan Pappé; Israeli journalists Max Blumenthal and Gideon Levy; professor, writer, activist, and presidential candidate Cornel West; author, journalist, and Pulitzer Prize winner Chris Hedges; columnist for *The Guardian* and international best-selling author Naomi Klein; world-class freedom fighter, author Angela Y. Davis; international consumer advocate, lawyer, and freedom fighter Ralph Nader; and over a hundred members of the United Nations, especially South Africa, which took the charge of genocide to the International Court of Justice, which it accepted.

It was 2 a.m. on January 16, 2024, a day after we had published Jonathan Tilove's book, *Along Martin Luther King*, an insightful look at the main streets in Black America named after Dr. King with photographs by Michael Falco, that I could not rest. Sleep just would not come. I kept thinking of what I had witnessed over the previous three months, thousands upon thousands of Palestinian babies, children, young people, their parents, grandparents, aunts, uncles, and others enduring death with no end of tragedies in sight. The next morning, I called Marc Lamont Hill[2] and suggested this book.

My insomnia was also due to deeply understanding the history of Israel in its brutal and volatile 76-year existence. The concept of the Jewish homeland, the Jewish state, grew in the mind of a man who many Jews of his time compared to Moses, Theodore Herzl (1860–1904). It was Herzl who turned Zionism into an international movement. He electrified the Jewish world with his oft-repeated declaration, "If you will it, it is no legend" (see Rabbi Joseph Telushkin's *Jewish Literacy: The Most Important Things to Know About Jewish Religion, Its People, and Its History*, reissued 2001). *Jewish Literacy* is an encyclopedia of original research and a must-read for Jewish and non-Jewish people who are seeking a one-volume view of Jewish history and culture. A part of my DNA has been the love of, protection, and education of children. We have built in Chicago three independent schools that were established in the 1960s, which today serve over 700 children through an African-centered education. Also, I am humanly aware of my own people's continued genocide, which we face daily in America. These domestic "war" crimes against Black people, starting with the Middle Passage, the enslavement of African people, the Civil War, Black Reconstruction, Black Codes, the Convict List Leasing System, Slave Patrols, Jim and Jane Crow Laws, Red Lining, Industrial Segregation, and technological job displacement, contribute to today's incarceration of over 2.5 million Black men, women, and young people in the nation's prisons, jails, and juvenile detention centers. The 13th Amendment of the U.S. Constitution legalized the continued enslavement of African Americans to be used to improve the livelihood and advancement of white people.

The current right-wing Zionist government, under the direction of Prime Minister Benjamin Netanyahu, is running an apartheid state that has largely lost credibility among nations after its response to the October 7th attack. Context: This existing "war," if it is to be named, did not start in 2023, but in 1917 with the Balfour Declaration (see *Mapping My Return: A Palestinian Memoir* by Selman Abu Sitta, 2016), which led to the 1948 Nakba "Catastrophe," the forced removal and deadly capture of Palestinian land by the Zionists and other Jews from Europe for a Jewish homeland. Over 750,000 women, children, and men were forced to abandon their homeland (see Robin D. G. Kelley's document entitled "1948: Israel, South Africa, and the Question of Genocide" in the addendums and the indispensable book by Ilan Pappé, *The Ethnic Cleansing of Palestine*, 2011 reprint).

I no doubt could anticipate—feel in my bones—the highly forceful and effective pro-Zionist narrative: the victimization of Israel and its unquestioned right to defend itself. There was little or no effort to tell the Palestinians' side of the coming and now existing "war." Only Hamas, without "history or provocation," has attacked Israel, massacred 1,200 humans, and kidnapped hundreds. This is a conservative description and, for me, unacceptable since I have studied and visited this part of the world in my extensive journey of struggle, political activism, teaching, writing, and institution-building over the past sixty years (see my poem, "The Secrets of the Victors," and comments in the poetry section). My response is not to be construed as anything but balanced. As I write now:

> *it is hard,*
> *it is difficult,*
> *it is an impossibility for a learned and history-made mind*
> *to be against a people, Jews, who have a centuries-long*
> *history of deep antisemitism, 20th century holocaust*
> *and unacknowledged deaths, history long destruction*
> *and displacement, struggles with outside madness*
> *and marches that help define a people,*
> *their lives have experienced poison breath,*
> *polluted water and new definitions of horror.*
>
> *yet, as some of them repeat and impose*
> *their history, anger and deaths upon another*
> *dependent and defenseless people, Palestinians,*
> *in today's times, in today's secondly moments*

acting as if another people's babies,
children, young people, women and elderly
slow walkers are THE enemy, as they also fight
against mass population displacement, ignorance,
statelessness from their culture and homeland.

It was art, primarily, poetry of all traditions, that taught me, as a young Black man, not to hate. Gwendolyn Brooks, Dudley Randall, and Robert Hayden helped inform the interior of my young warrior life. The brilliant poetic activism of Allen Ginsberg, the many layers of Studs Terkel, Robert Pinsky, and Gerald Stern, and the absolute dedicated genius of Adrienne Rich also helped me to formulate my life through their acts of human-centeredness and confirmation that poetry was the correct destination that led me to unconditionally love and care for all children. Adrienne Rich, in her acceptance remarks upon receiving the National Book Foundation Medal in 2006, states:

> I am both a poet and one of the "everybodies" of my country. I live, in poetry and daily experience, with manipulated fear, ignorance, cultural confusion, and social antagonism huddling together on the fault line of an empire. In my lifetime I've seen the breakdown of rights and citizenship with ordinary "everybodies," poets or not, have left politics to a political class bent on shoveling the elemental resources, the public commons of the entire world into private control. Where democracy has been left to the raiding of "acknowledged" legislators, the highest bidders. In short, to a criminal element ... Democratic[s] and Republican[s]— have backed dictatorships against popular movements abroad; as their covert agencies, through torture and assassination, through supplied weapons and military training, have propped up repressive parties and regimes ... fascistic methods, the subversion of civil and human rights ... a self-righteous false innocence, eyes shut to our own scenario, our body politic's internal bleeding (Adrienne Rich, *Poetry & Commitment*, 2007).

We all do what we have been taught to do. Hatred of others is a learned activity. White Supremacy, White Nationalism, White Christian Nationalism, and Christian and Jewish Zionism are not only political and deadly, but also cultural. And yes, within the Islamic tradition and culture, there is similar madness, with people also making deadly statements and committing horrific actions. However, it is the West, with the United States and its allies, that is in total support of Israel. As the current and only empire in the world, the United States' unquestioned backing of Israel has positioned Israel in the minds of many as the nation's fifty-first state. What is not being acknowledged enough is that President Joe Biden, Secretary of State Antony Blinken, Secretary of Defense Lloyd Austin, as well as Senate Head Chuck Schumer and Minority Leader of the U.S. House of Representatives Hakeem Jefferies, must also share the weight of this mass slaughter on their watch. And the invitation from both Republicans and Democrats to have Prime Minister Benjamin Netanyahu speak to both houses of Congress at the end of July 2024 truly was an abomination. Allowing Netanyahu's statement of lies to Congress and the nation to go unchallenged erased what little moral high ground the U.S. possessed. Most certainly, since 9/11, the right-wing of this nation and the state of Israel have been able to use the charge "terrorism" to justify most of its military acts against Palestinians and others; the Iraq and Afghanistan wars are the deadliest examples of the U.S. recent misuse of power. President Biden warned Netanyahu not to make the same "mistakes" that this country made in its response to Gaza. Nonetheless, Israel's requests for greater resources in the continued occupation, demolition of Palestine, and serious oppression of its people, especially children, are automatically given carte blanche by the United States.

Jen Marlowe, in an article that was published in *The Nation*, "The Children of Gaza" (7/20/2015), details the "permanent war" that Israel reigns over occupied Palestine daily. Israel controls most of Palestine, its water, electricity, roads, equipment flow, food flow, education space, and one can go on and on. Marlowe points out that the major conflicts of Operation Hot Winter (also called Operation Warm Winter, February 2008), Operation Cast Lead (also known as the Gaza Massacre, December 2008), Operation Returning Echo (March 2012), Operation Pillar of Defense (November 2012), and Operation Protective Edge (July 2014) produced unimaginable material destruction and cost the lives of over 3,826 Palestinian children and adults and 93 Israeli children and adults. Ilan Pappé, in his book *On Palestine* (2015), defined "the Israel policy toward the Gaza Strip as incremental genocide." This is not an overstatement. Yet, due to the United States' all-out support of Israel, history may not record this sorrowful tale accurately. In addition, Noam Chomsky offers his educated, long view in an op-ed published by *Truthout*:

> When Israel is on "good behavior," more than two Palestinian children are killed every week, a pattern that goes back over fourteen years. The underlying cause is the criminal occupation and the programs to reduce Palestinian life to bare survival in Gaza, while Palestinians are restricted to unviable canons in the West Bank and Israel takes over what

it wants, all in gross violation of international law and explicit Security Council resolutions, not to speak of minimal decency. And it will continue—as long as it is supported by Washington and tolerated by Europe—to our everlasting shame (Chomsky, "Gaza's Torment, Israel's Crimes, Our Responsibilities" *Truthout,* July 14, 2014).

U.S. support for Israel is hardly the only source of anti-Americanism in the Arabic and Islamic worlds, and making this particular situation less confrontational would not remove all sources of friction between these countries and the United States. Examining the consequences of Israel's treatment of the Palestinians and tacit U.S. support of these policies is not to deny the presence of genuine anti-Semitism in various Arabic countries and Western nations, or the fact that groups and governments in these societies sometimes fan these attitudes and use the Israel-Palestine conflict to divert attention from their own mistakes and crimes. Rather, the point is simply that the United States pays a substantial price for supporting Israel so consistently. This posture fuels hostility toward the United States in the Middle East, motivates anti-American freedom fighters and extremists, and aids them in recruiting anti-American fighters. The authoritarian governments in the region also use American influences as an all-too-convenient scapegoat for their own failings, which makes it harder for Washington to convince potential supporters to confront extremists in their own countries.

According to John J. Mearsheimer and Stephen M. Walt's book, *The Israel Lobby and U.S. Foreign Policy* (2007), "When it comes to fighting terrorism, in short, U.S. and Israeli interests are not identical. Backing Israel against the Palestinians makes winning the war on terror harder, not easier, and the 'partner against terror' rationale does not provide a compelling justification for unconditional U.S. support." The publication of their essay, which has expanded into a book, contributed to changing the conversation in America and much of the western world in our understanding of Israel's relationship and alliance with one of the top lobbying efforts in the world, the American Israel Public Affairs Committee (AIPAC). In the May/June 2024 issue of *Capitol Hill Citizen,* the lead story is "Citizens Push Back Against AIPAC Dominance: Tracking Lobbyists' Million Dollar Club" by Russell Mokhiber, in which he states, "In April 2024 Congress overwhelmingly passed and President Biden signed a military aid bill that provides 95 billion in war aid—including 61 billion to Ukraine, 8 billion to Taiwan, and 26 billion to Israel—in effect a genocide tax on the American people."

Also worth noting, the *New York Times* (the so-called newspaper of record is also the paper of the U.S. empire within the nation) editorial and opinion pages led by Thomas L. Friedman, David Brooks, Bret Stephens, and Nicholas Kristof immediately took the side of Israel and the IDF without any insight into the why of the Hamas attack. One should review the work of Professor Rashid Khalidi, one of the few experts on the faculty of Columbia University who has made Palestine his lifelong work. His latest book, The *Hundred Years' War on Palestine: A History of Settler Colonialism and Resistance, 1917–2017* (2020), puts the Palestinian fight for justice in a historical and human perspective. A must read if indeed we are seeking a full and accurate history of that troubled land.

*explain how 2.3 million humans living within a
land mass of twenty-five by five miles
of an "open air prison," actually a modern concentration
death camp, is to escape air bombs,
rockets, raining missiles, sniper fire,
morally and ethically conflicted young IDF warriors
unaware of their own death madness and
marchers now forcing a recent defenseless people
who will build their own stories, histories
and memories of open-eyed destruction
of hospitals becoming graveyards, schools
becoming unrecognizable and unusable brick,
as we go into enduring "war" against all universities,
libraries, schools, cultural centers
and medical facilities no longer exist,*

*bodies, bodies, and bodies
still unearthed and missing while searching
for water, electricity, fuel and healing spaces,
searching for food, more water, medical care,
hope and recovery spaces, 2.3 million
people, populated by over half babies, children,
and young people in a twenty-five by five miles
of occupied land that is totally, absolutely,
and without a doubt, controlled by recently arrived
Zionist death bringers, and killers who settled
a newly created nation less than 76 years old
that is now and now, governed by a corrupt
and incompetent Zionist leadership
afraid of its own shadow, past and future
in the existing dark and light of history
and deadly politics making deals
with the devils that they have become.*

To be accurate, the *New York Times*, in a very detailed and unusual essay in its magazine of May 19, 2024, "Israel's Extremist Takeover" by Rowen Bergman and Mark Mazzetti, answers many of the questions and does put into context the whys of this "war." Also, Megan K. Stacks' essay "In Israel, the Darkness is Everywhere" reveals that much of Israel today is accepting and encouraging the "war" with Hamas (*New York Times*, 5/18/24).

When we undertook this project, there was a great possibility of our being accused of being anti-Semitic. However, in these volatile times, the charge of anti-Semitism has been misused to divert or scare off any serious criticism of the state of Israel and its Zionist founders and direct rulership. The best examples of this tactic consist of much of the coverage of the student protests at many of the universities in the U.S. and around the world. Media makers have been attempting to change the conversation from genocide in Gaza to the rekindling of local, national, and international anti-Semitism (more later).

The reference list that follows this essay contains a substantial number of books that give an accurate historical record of the founding of the state of Israel. Several Jewish journals, such as *Moment, Commentary,* and the digital publication, *The Forward,* and *Jewish Currents,* among others, give us an inside view of the very complicated Jewish world. The February 2024 issue of *Harper's* magazine's lead essay is "Israel's War Within: The Battle for a Country's Soul" by Bernard Avishai. The April 2024 issue of the *Atlantic* leads with "The End of the Golden Age," by Franklin Fore, which explores anti-Semitism on the right and left, and the May/June 2024 issue of *Foreign Affairs* has the critically important essay by Tom Segev, "Israel's Forever War: The Long History of Managing—Rather Than Solving—The Conflict," all of which add substantially to our understanding of the current "war."

Several books that also come to mind are Gideon Levy's *The Punishment of Gaza* (2010); Amira Hass' *Drinking the Sea at Gaza: Days and Nights in a Land Under Siege* (1996, translation 1999); and Ilan Pappé's *The Ethnic Cleansing of Palestine*. In addition, Ilan Pappé's recently published book, *Lobbying for Zionism on Both Sides of the Atlantic* (Oneworld, 2024), is the most up-to-date analysis of the Christian, British, and American lobbyists for Israel before and after the Holocaust—a critical study from a Jewish historian who has devoted his life's work to the subject.

However, to clearly understand the human and cultural, psychological trauma, economic disaster, land grab by Zionists, absolute family destruction and devastation, and the betrayal of the Arab and international communities and the daily unanswered questions and sorrow endured by children, their parents, and extended family trying to protect them, this struggle needed a singular voice. There are several books that I list in the references, but the one book I feel is most accessible to all readers is *We Could Have Been Friends, My Father and I: A Palestinian Memoir* (2022) by Raja Shehadeh. Also, to understand Hamas in its historical, political, military, economic, cultural and governing aspects, Tareq Baconi's *Hamas Contained: A History of Palestinian Resistance* (2024) is a must read, as well as *Rise and Kill First: A Secret History of Israel's Targeted Assassinations* (2019) by Ronen Bergman.

Two major journals that cover the Middle East and concentrate on the Israeli occupation of Palestine are *Mondoweiss: News & Opinion About Palestine, Israel & the United States*, and the *Washington Report on Middle East Affairs*. In July 2024, Delinda Hanley, executive editor of the *Washington Report*, was interviewed on the Ralph Nader radio program, where she stated that "the magazine gives you material you can't get anywhere else." She further stated "A while back, they printed the vile anti-Semitic, racist remarks against Palestinian Semites by high Israeli officials, people who are heads of political parties, ministers, prime ministers, verbatim, some of the most vile epithets that can be hurled against any ethnic group. One was by the head of a political party, who referred to Palestinian newborns as snakes coming out ... and we should go after their mothers." As the interview continued, Hanley made it very clear that the Washington Report publishes what the mainstream press will not. The first two editions of 2024 are necessary readings of the coverage of the present crisis. One of the remarkable interviews in the May 2024 issue is with an undertaker in Gaza, notes Delinda Hanley:

> His name is Abu Jawad. He's 64-years-old and he was a farmer. He would get up and deal with his olive oil trees and produce olive oil. And then, October 7th came, and the questions was, who's going to bury all these dead civilians? And he volunteered, working 6a.m. to 6p.m. with four other displaced Palestinians, and they weren't being paid. It's something that he did, and he prayed and cried throughout the whole day. He said, "I buried about 10 times more people during this war than I did across my 27 years as an undertaker. The least was thirty people a day. The most was 800 people a day. Since October 7th, I buried more than 17,000 people." That's in two cemeteries to indicate how vast the undercount is in this genocidal war that Israel has inflicted on a defenseless population, as Gideon Levy once called the Palestinians of Gaza. And the official figure now is just under 38,000

throughout all of Gaza being killed by the Israeli military. He's buried 17,000 himself. I think the real figure is about 250,000 dead.

I would also like to bring to your attention the following essays in the *New York Review of Books*: "Israel: The Way Out" (May 9, 2024) and "A Bitter Season in the West Bank" (December 7, 2023), both by David Shulman; "Is Israel Committing Genocide?" by Aryeh Neier (June 6, 2024); and "No End Game in Gaza" by Fintan O'Toole (December 7, 2023), all critically important, each containing life-changing suggestions for Israelis and Palestinians. I also would highly recommend you keep up with the books on Jewish politics and culture featured in the *Jewish Review of Books*, which is published quarterly.

Finally, in 1988, Edward S. Herman and Noam Chomsky published a ground-shaking book, *Manufacturing Consent: The Political Economy of the Mass Media*, and in 2002 Noam Chomsky updated some of its key ideas in *Media Control: The Spectacular Achievement of Propaganda* (Seven Stories Press, 2002) where he writes:

> One conception of democracy has it that democratic society is one in which the public has the means to participate in some meaningful way in the management of their own affairs and the means of information are open and free…An alternative conception of democracy is that the public must be barred from managing of their own affairs and the means of information must be kept narrowly and rigidly controlled. That may sound like an odd conception of democracy, but it's important to understand that it is the prevailing conception. In fact, it has long been, not just in operation, but even in theory (*Media Control*).

Recently, two documentaries have appeared on the *YouTube* channel that highlight the democratic power of social media. *The Night Won't End* is a devastating account of the collective punishment, extermination, and genocide of primarily Gazan children and teenagers. The director of this important documentary is Kavitha Chekuru, and the film is produced by Al Jazeera's Fault Lines with independent journalist Sharif Abdel Kguddous, who helped to create with others this critically important, historically accurate account of the horrific killing of young people and independent journalists. *The Night Won't End* partially tells a story of how Israel's IDF are wiping out entire bloodlines and is a must see for anyone who is serious about what is happening today in the "killing" of the future in Gaza. The film is dedicated to the 150 journalists who have been murdered as a result of covering the "war" in Gaza.

The second documentary is entitled *How U.S News Media Manufactured Anti-Semitism on Campuses* and appeared on *Backspace,* edited with commentary by Sana Saeed. Ms. Saeed gives us clear language, imagery, and insight into how the super-rich and mass media conglomerates changed the conversation and emphasis from the fact of genocide in Gaza to that of anti-Semitism in the United States and around the world. She focuses on the role of Jewish and non-Jewish students at universities and colleges across the nation. The documentary makes clear the role of BDS (Boycott, Divestment, and Sanctions), which is over 15 years old, bringing us up to the present regarding its effect and importance as a non-violent protest strategy. She highlights the critical impact of mass media such as Tik Tok. *Democracy Now!* with Amy Goodman must be credited with keeping her viewers aware of the day-to-day atrocities in Gaza and elsewhere in the world.

Indeed, this is a teaching moment. This book, *For Gaza's Children,* is our contribution to truth and justice for Palestinians, especially children and young people, as well as for liberated Israelis who do not agree with its corrupt, ruling Zionist-Israeli government. As of today, Israel is justifiably on the UN "blacklist" of countries that harm children, and we must be aware that the International Court of Justice has issued arrest warrants for Benjamin Netanyahu and others. The most recent number of children's deaths easily exceeds 20,000.

Gazan land, which nobody is making any more of: destroyed
schools, mosques, gathering places: destroyed.
homes, libraries, cultural centers, farms: destroyed.
hospitals, stores, universities, colleges: destroyed.
roads, sewer systems, electrical grids, greenhouses: destroyed.
what used to serve the people in Palestine is no longer
in Gaza as well as tens of thousands of Palestinians.
ethnic and cultural annihilation
death's death, the Zionist's "Greater Israel"
whitening out your signature and children's smiles
silencing your educators, historians, musicians,
village storytellers, librarians and journalists, all
disregarding your name, erasing your breath,
vacating your existence, the Abraham Accords, (2020).
these babies and young
people these daughters and
sons, these developing
geniuses
at the apex of their calling
would demand a renewed

commitment to smiles, safe territory
and the noticing of simple pleasures: grass, sun,
the unhurried walk of the elderly,
the magical laughter of the
innocent, dancing to the melodies
of love, security and freedom,
embracing the education of young
seekers, wisdom chasers, the taste
of fresh grapes, watermelon,
peaches, dates and water.

as unthinkable as it seems today, we remain
the wind, ocean and sun of their missing lives.
we are the answers to their unasked questions
we must be the on-goings, get-ups
and critical yeses of future days.
for these are our babies, too,
as Israel immorally cleanses Gaza,
and creates a criminal-infused history questioned
by the world and its own children.
for Gaza's children,
they are our children too!

References

Abu Sitta, Salman. *Mapping My Return: A Palestinian Memoir.* The American University in Cairo Press, 2016.

Alexander, Michelle. T*he New Jim Crow: Mass Incarceration in the Age of Colorblindness.* The New Press, 2010.

Angel, Arielle, editor. "After October 7." Jewish Currents, 2024.

Aslan, Reza. *A Kids Book about Israel & Palestine.* A Kids Book About, Inc., 2024.

Baconi, Tareq. *Hamas Contained: The Rise and Pacification of Palestinian Resistance* (Stanford Studies in Middle Eastern and Islamic Societies and Cultures) 1st Edition. Stanford University Press, 2022.

Beinart, Peter. *The Crisis of Zionism.* Picador, 2012.

Blumenthal, Max. *The 51 Day War.* Leftword Press, 2015.

Caridi, Paola. *HAMAS: From Resistance to Regime.* Seven Stories Press, revised and updated edition translated by Andrea Teti, 2023.

Carter, Jimmy. Palestine: *Peace Not Apartheid.* Simon & Schuster, 2006.

Charles, Mark and Soong-Chan, Rah. *Unsettling Truths: Ongoing Dehumanizing Legacy of the Doctrine of Discovery.* IVP Publishing, 2019.

Chomsky, Noam. *The Fateful Triangle: The United States, Israel and the Palestinians.* South End Press, 1983.

—Media Control, Second Edition: *The Spectacular Achievements of Propaganda* (Open Media Series). Seven Stories Press, 2002.

Churchill, Ward. *A Little Matter of Genocide: Holocaust and Denial in the Americas 1492 to the Present.* City Lights Books, 1997.

Cohen, Joshua. *The Netanyahus.* Fitzcarraldo Editions, 2021.

Cramer, Richard Ben. *How Israel Lost.* Simon and Schuster, 2004.

Darwish, Mahmoud. *Mural.* Translated by John Berger and Reman Aminai. Verso, 2024.

___. *Palestine As Metaphor.* Translated by Amira El-Zein and Carolyn Forchē. Olive Branch Press, 2019.

___. *In the Presence of Absence.* Translated by Sinan Antoon. Archipelage, 2011.

Davis, Angela Y. *Freedom is a Constant Struggle: Ferguson, Palestine, and the Foundation of a Movement.* Haymarket Books, 2016.

Dobbie, Joan, and Grace Beeler. *Before There Is Nowhere to Stand: Palestine/Israel: Poets Respond to the Struggle.* Lost Horse Press, 2012. Du Bois, W.E.B. Black Reconstruction in America: 1860-1880. Russell & Russell, 1935.

Du, Bois, W.E.B. *Black Reconstruction in America, 1860-1880.* Russell & Russell, 1935.

—*The World and Africa.* Viking Press, 1946, 1947.

Elizur, Yuval, and Lawrence Malkin. *The War Within.* Bloomsbury Academic, 2013.

Erakat, Noura. *JUSTICE for SOME: Law and the Question of Palestine.* Stanford University Press, 2019.

Fersko, Rabbi Diana. *We Need to Talk about Antisemitism.* First Edition, Seal Press, 2023.

Finkelstein, Norman. "This Time We Went Too Far": Truth and Consequences of the Gaza Invasion. OR Books, 2010.

—. *The Holocaust Industry.* Verso, 2000.

—. *Gaza: An Inquest into Its Martyrdom.* University of California Press, 2018.

Gradowski, Zalmen. *The Last Consolation Vanished: The Testimony of a Sonderkommando in Auschwitz.* Edited by Arnold I Davidson and Philippe Mesnard. Translated by Rubye Monet. The University of Chicago Press, 2022.

Hass, Amira. *Drinking the Sea at Gaza: Days and Nights in a Land under Siege.* Translated by Elana Wesley and Maxine Kaufman-Lacusta. Holt, 1996.

Hedges, Chris. *American Fascists: The Christian Right and the War on America.* Free Press, 2006.

Herman, Edward S. and Chomsky, Noam. *Manufacturing Consent: The Political Economy of the Mass Media.* Pantheon Books, 2002.

Hill, Marc Lamont, and Mitchell Plitnick. *Except for Palestine: The Limits of Progressive Politics.* New Press, 2021.

Hitchens, Christopher, and Edward W. Said. *Blaming the Victims: Spurious*

Scholarship and the Palestinian Question. Verso, 2001.

Hixson, Walter. *Architects of Repression.* Institute for Research Middle Eastern Policy Incorporated, 2021.

—. *Imperialism and War.* Institute for Research, 2021.

Horn, Dara. *People Love Dead Jews: Reports from a Haunted Present.* Norton, 2021.

Jacobs, Charles, and Avi Goldwasser, editors. *Betrayal: The Failure of American Jewish Leadership.* Wicked Son, 2023.

Jiryis, Fida. *Stranger in My Own Land: Palestine, Israel and One Family's Story of Home.* Hurst, 2023.

Kennard, Matt. *Silent Coup: How Corporations Overthrew Democracy.* Bloomsbury Academic, 2023.

— *The Racket: A Rogue Reporter vs. The Masters of the Universe.* Zed, 2015.

Khalidi, Rashid. *Hundred Years' War on Palestine: A History of Settler Colonialism and Resistance, 1917-2017.* Picador, 2021.

—. *The Iron Cage: The Story of the Palestinian Struggle for Statehood.* Oneworld, 2006.

Kline, Naomi. *Doppelganger: A Trip into the Mirror World.* Farrar, Straus & Giroux, 2023.

Levit, Daphna. *Wrestling with Zionism: Jewish Voices of Dissent.* Olive Branch Press, an Imprint of Interlink Publishing Group, Inc, 2020.

Levy, Gideon. *The Punishment of Gaza.* Verso, 2010.

Mearsheimer, John J., and Stephen M. Walt. *The Israel Lobby and US Foreign Policy.* Penguin, 2007.

Moushabeck, Hannah (author) Madooch, Reem (illustrator). *Homeland: My Family Dreams of Palestine.* Chronicle Books, 2023.

Pappé, Ilan. *The Ethnic Cleansing of Palestine.* Oneworld, 2006.

–*Lobbying for Zionism on Both Sides of the Atlantic.* Oneworld, 2024.

–*Ten Myths About Israel.* Verso, 2017.

Patterson, William L. (editor). *We Charge Genocide: The Crime of Government Against the Negro People* (with preface by Ossie Davis, 3rd edition). International Publishers, 1970.

Reinhart, Tanya. *Israel/Palestine: How to End the War of 1948* (2nd edition). Seven Stories Press, 2002.

Rich, Adrienne. *Poetry & Commitment: An Essay.* Norton, 2007.

Rothchild, Alice. *Condition Critical: Life and Death in Israel/Palestine.* Just World Books, 2016.

Rutherford, Ward. *Genocide: The Jews in Europe 1939-45.* Ballantine, 1973.

Sabbagh, Karl. *Palestine: A Personal History.* Grove, 2006.

Sacco, Joe. *Footnotes in Gaza.* Metropolitan, 2009.

Said, Edward. *Orientalism.* Vintage, 1979.

—. *The Question of Palestine*. Vintage, 1979.

Salaita, Steven. *Uncivil Rites: Palestine and the Limits of Academic Freedom*. Haymarket, 2015.

Sand, Shlomo. *How I Stopped Being a Jew*. Verso, 2014.

—. *The Invention of the Land of Israel*. Verso, 2012.

Shehadeh, Raja. *What Does Israel Fear from Palestine?* Other Press, 2024.

Shehadeh, Raja. *We Could Have Been Friends, My Father and I: A Palestinian Memoir*. Other Press, 2023.

Shlaim, Avi. *The Iron Wall: Israel and the Arab World* (Updated and Expanded). Norton, 2014.

–*Three Worlds: Memoirs of an Arab Jew*. Oneworld, 2023.

Stanley, Jason. *Erasing History: How Fascists Rewrite the Past to Control The Future*. One Signal Publishers / ATRIA, 2024.

Suárez, Thomas. *Palestine Hijacked: How Zionism Forged an Apartheid State from River to Sea*. Olive Branch Press, 2023.

Telushkin, Joseph. *Jewish Literacy: The Most Important Things to Know about the Jewish Religion, Its People, and Its History*. William Morrow, 2001.

Valley, Eli, and Peter Beinart. *Diaspora Boy: Comics on Crisis in America and Israel*. OR Books, 2017.

Winstanley, Asa. *Weaponising Anti-Semitism: How the Israel Lobby Brought Down Jeremy Corbyn*. OR Books, LLC, 2023.

Final Notes:

The enormous amount of money at AIPAC's fingertips was, in the first and final analysis, responsible for the defeat of two Black Congress people in their 2024 primaries, Jamaal Bowman of New York, and Cori Bush of Missouri. As integral parts of the so-called "squad," their voices criticizing the "war" in Gaza and opposition against the funding of Israel's genocide was the final blow prompting AIPAC to donate millions to their opposition (see "In Congresswoman's Defeat, Israel Lobby Shows It's Clout," *New York Times*, front page - 8/9/24, by Luke Broadwater).

Also, it is widely known by those who study the Israeli / Palestinian conflicts that Prime Minister Netanyahu has been secretly funding Hamas and Palestinians. In the December 11, 2023, issue of *The Telegraph*, Nataliya Vasileva, published "Israel Sent Suitcases of Cash into Gaza for Years Despite Concerns About Funding Hamas." This support for Hamas pushed the former right-wing Defense Minister, Avigdor Lieberman, to resign in November of 2018. Lieberman was quoted in the article: "The Prime Minister planned to stay in power at any cost." Many experts feel this led directly to the October 7th attack.

Please view "Starving Gaza" / Fault Lines / Al Jazeera films, English (2024), a film by Hind Hassan and others.

Where Are Palestinian Children's Human Rights?

Lara Friedman

I last visited the Gaza Strip in November 2014, where I stayed at the Al Deira Hotel. That lovely hotel—demolished by Israel in the current war—was briefly made famous on July 16, 2014. On that day an Israeli gunboat fired at a group of Palestinian boys playing soccer on the beach just outside the hotel. The attack, witnessed by numerous journalists staying at the hotel, killed a 9-year-old, two 10-year-olds, and an 11-year-old. The Israeli response following its own investigation? The deaths were a tragedy but "the attack process in question accorded with Israeli domestic law and international law requirements."

During my visit I saw first-hand the aftermath of the July-August 2014 Israeli war on Gaza, which Israel dubbed "Operation Protective Edge." I thought I was prepared, having followed the war closely in real time from afar, but coming face to face with entire neighborhoods reduced to ruins, with people still living among the rubble, was crushing. Yet, that was nothing compared to meeting the people of Gaza. They welcomed me (and yes, they knew I was Jewish and working at that time for a liberal Zionist organization). They introduced me to their children with pride and talked to me with almost unbearable calm and dignity of their losses and pain. And they conveyed, frankly, their bafflement, anger, and sense of total abandonment following a 50-day Israeli military offensive that killed at least 1,391 civilians, of which, according to B'Tselem, "180 were babies, toddlers, and children under the age of six. Another 346 were children from age six through seventeen."

The children of Gaza whom I met on that visit have never left my mind. Most of all I recall my visit to a UN girls' school, where the teachers and students showed me around and invited me to sit in on a class with students aged around 11 or 12. The students explained proudly that they were studying human rights, conflict resolution, and tolerance. As the class progressed, one of the students stood up to ask me a question. With the preternatural poise and maturity common in children who have had their childhood stolen by catastrophe or trauma, she asked me (in careful, perfect English that I remember so well, this is close to a direct quote): "I am a child. I've lived most of my life under Israeli blockade. I've lived through three Israeli wars on Gaza. I've seen friends and family die, their homes destroyed. I've studied human rights and I want to know: what about us? Where are our human rights?" She clearly knew, even as she posed the question, that I had no response.

23

Returning to the U.S., I told friends and colleagues—and anyone else who would listen—about what I had seen and heard in Gaza. I talked about the terrible toll on children imposed by Israel's years-long blockade and by Israeli military assaults. I talked about the hopelessness and anger among Palestinians that comes from knowing, from a very young age, that the world has turned its back on them and that their lives don't count. I talked about the moral imperative to demand that the U.S. government use its leverage to compel Israel to end the blockade, to pressure Israel to cease violations of Palestinian rights everywhere, and to restore a credible horizon for ending Israeli occupation and achieving Palestinian freedom and self-determination.

Many of my interlocutors agreed. Many more seemed conflicted—sympathetic to Palestinian suffering but overwhelmed by the enormity of the challenge of changing the status quo. But too many, including on Capitol Hill and in the U.S. government, took refuge in the all-too-familiar approach of blaming the victims: Yes, what is happening to children in Gaza is terrible, but so long as Hamas exists, and until Palestinians embrace Israel's right to exist as a Jewish state, there is nothing we or anyone can do to help them.

How is this possible? How can people have so little care for the lives and welfare of human beings, and in particular children? How is it that support for Israel translates to utter indifference to, if not outright contempt for, human life when that life is Palestinian? How is it that long before the October 7, 2023, Hamas attacks that were the catalyst for Israel's current military assault on Gaza, it had already become accepted in the public debate to view human lives in Gaza, including children's, as presumptively legitimate military targets or collateral-damage-waiting-to-happen? How is it that the world has normalized Israeli military doctrine that boils down to a never-ending fight to compel Palestinians in Gaza—most of whom are refugees from land that is today Israel—to acquiesce to their own oppression, dispossession, erasure, and dehumanization? How has the world come to accept the Israeli worldview described by my friend Danny Seidemann (speaking about Israeli policy in Jerusalem), which holds that "the birth of an Israeli child is a simcha [Hebrew for "joy"] and the birth of a Palestinian child is a demographic threat"---or translated to the Gaza context, that the birth of a Palestinian child is a terrorist threat?

Since October 7, 2023, this blame-the-victim framing is back with a vengeance. As soon as someone starts talking about Israel injuring or killing thousands of Palestinian civilians in Gaza, including children, the We-Stand-With-Israel hallelujah choir sings, "Hamas started it! So whoever Israel kills, Hamas bears all responsibility for those deaths!!"

Do they hear themselves? This logic is a moral obscenity, absolving

Israel of both agency and responsibility for literally anything it does in Gaza. If normalized, this logic will validate a new doctrine of war-making for the entire world according to which there are no limits to the harms that may be inflicted on civilians. Indeed, this logic renders the status of "civilian" irrelevant; so long as the party waging war claims the other side "started it," they are allowed to disclaim responsibility for every man, woman, and child they injure or kill. Do supporters of Israel believe a world that embraces this doctrine of war will be safer for themselves and their children? For Jews anywhere? Or even for Israel?

And as Israel is recorded (indeed, as its own soldiers serially record themselves, and post the videos on TikTok) committing war crimes against Palestinian civilians, the same hallelujah choir sings: "they voted for Hamas!" Or as Israel's own president, Isaac Herzog said, "It is an entire nation out there that is responsible…It is not true this rhetoric about civilians not being aware, not involved. It's absolutely not true. They could have risen up. They could have fought against that evil regime which took over Gaza in a coup d'etat."

Do they hear themselves? This argument is morally depraved. Even if they had voted for Hamas, and even if they failed to overthrow Hamas, that doesn't make them responsible for its actions. To suggest otherwise is to mirror the rationale employed by terrorists everywhere to justify attacking civilians, including the 9/11 terrorists who in effect held all Americans responsible for what they saw as the crimes of our government, and saw every American as, therefore, a legitimate target. It is also disconnected from reality. Do facts matter? The majority of Palestinians in Gaza were either not born yet or were not old enough to vote the last time there were elections in Palestine (in January 2006). Of the people in Gaza who were old enough to vote, most did not vote for Hamas. Rather, Hamas (or as they were called in that election, the Party of Change and Reform) won a plurality of the vote across all of Palestine; in Gaza they won less than 50% of the vote in all but one district.

When I was a child, I often heard adults—whose worldview was shaped both by the Holocaust and by anti-Semitism they had faced in the U.S. —gravely state, "the test of any country is how it treats its Jews." Later I came to understand that this was a Jewish-centered take on a quote that is attributed (though there is much debate on this) to both Hubert Humphrey and Mahatma Gandhi. That quote, in its various formulations, boils down to this: The measure of a society (or a civilization) is how it treats its weakest (or most vulnerable) members. In the minds of my parents and grandparents and others of their generations, it was an indisputable fact that the Jews are and forever will be the most vulnerable people in any society, anywhere in the world.

Yet today, we—the Jewish people—are by no intellectually honest measure the most vulnerable population anywhere in the world. And while Israel faces threats, its Jewish citizens, living in a state that prioritizes their interests, backed by one of the world's most powerful armies, enjoying strong support from the U.S. and most of the world, are certainly not the most vulnerable population living between the Jordan River and the Mediterranean Sea.

In contrast, the Palestinians, by an accident of geography and history, are arguably the world's most politically and historically inconvenient people—crushed between the millstones of the end of the colonial era and the world's post-Holocaust embrace of Zionism. As such, they are, by any intellectually honest measure, among the most vulnerable people in the world. This is especially true of those living between the Jordan River and the Mediterranean Sea, where Palestinians face relentless, almost unimaginable adversity, day after day, year after year, at the hands of successive Israeli governments who view their very existence as anathema to Israeli interests and objectives in this land. They persist, no matter that they were dispossessed of their lands and homes in 1948. Yet, Palestinians persist, generation after generation, refusing to disappear or give up on their rights and humanity. They persist, disenfranchised and deprived of basic rights under Israeli military occupation since 1967. They persist as second-class citizens in Israel, their status a testament to the racism inherent in Israel's democracy, even towards its own citizens. They persist, as conditional "residents" in Jerusalem, notwithstanding the fact that the city has been home to their families for generations dating back before 1948.

In almost any other context, the world would honor and celebrate a people that holds on to their collective humanity and preserves their collective history and identity in the face of such adversity. In almost any other context, the world would stand with and seek to defend these extraordinarily vulnerable people. But thanks to the aforementioned accident of geography and history, Palestinians instead face even more adversity.

Israel and its supporters around the globe, including in the US government and Congress, never cease to attack and delegitimize any effort to secure for Palestinians the same rights and protections granted under international law to people everywhere, or to hold Israel accountable for its actions against them. Protest via boycotts is decried as "economic terrorism." Efforts to obtain support at the UN are slammed as "diplomatic terrorism." Media coverage documenting violations of Palestinian rights is dismissed as "journalistic terrorism." Scholarly work critical of Israel is condemned as "academic terrorism." Efforts to find recourse in the justice system of various countries is slammed as "lawfare." Aid for Palestinian refugees is attacked as "support for terrorism." And a common through line connecting all these attacks: defaming Palestinians and Palestine rights activists as anti-Semites and supporters of terrorism for the sin of giving voice to Palestinian grievances, or the Palestinian lived historical narrative vis-a-vis Israel and Zionism, or Palestinian aspirations for justice.

As I write this essay at the end of January 2024, Israel has (so far) killed more than 26,000 Palestinians in the Gaza Strip since October 6, 2023. The vast majority of these are civilians, and over half of them are children, with the numbers rising every day, sometimes by the hundreds. There are thousands more dead or dying Palestinians trapped under collapsed buildings, and thousands more injured, crippled, and dying for lack of medical treatment. Hundreds if not thousands of children have lost one or both parents, and a horrific new humanitarian category has been coined in this Gaza war: WCNSF—"wounded child, no surviving family" —wounded children with no living relatives left to care for them or in some cases to even identify them. More than 2 million people are at this time being deliberately starved and deprived of health care. More than 1 million human beings have been displaced, most multiple times, and are today without adequate shelter in the dead of winter.

This reality—which aligns closely with intent expressed in statements by Israel officials from the earliest days of this war to the present—lays bare a central truth about this war: Israel's response to Hamas's brutal October 7 attack is not and never was merely about freeing hostages taken by Hamas, who absolutely must be freed. And it is not and never was merely about restoring deterrence or ensuring that Hamas would never again be able to repeat its October 7 attack on Israel. Rather, a key objective of Israel's war on Gaza, or arguably the key objective of this war, is to fundamentally change not just the rules of the game with respect to Israel's Gaza policy, but to substitute a whole new game board. On this new game board, Gaza's Palestinians—their civilization and their lives, including their children's lives —are to the greatest possible extent diminished, if not entirely eradicated.

All of this today is clear, even if those with the power to restrain Israel prefer—for reasons of self-interest, or anti-Palestinian racism, or political cowardice—to close their eyes and only look up when the genocide and ethnic cleansing of Palestinians in Gaza is in the rearview mirror. And the day after Israel deems its objectives achieved, they can look forward to celebrating their benevolence as white saviors, ready to provide subsistence aid to desperate Palestinians who survive the war—almost all of whom will be destitute refugees (like their parents and grandparents were in 1948), whether allowed to remain inside Gaza or forced out.

It has become trendy these days, when learning something new, for people to quip, "I was today years old when I found out X." Assuming the remarkable girl I met at that UN school in Gaza back in 2014 is still alive, she would now be in her early 20s. In the twisted time-counting forced on her generation, that makes her 6-wars-old—having lived through Israeli assaults in December 2008-January 2009, November 2012, July-August 2014, May 2021, August 2022, and the current genocide underway since October 2023. And she would have lived almost her entire life under Israeli blockade.

"What about us? Where are our human rights?" she asked me back in 2014. I didn't have an answer for her then. And I don't have one now.

Rafeek* (For Paul & Nada)

Brian Gilmore

There are Palestinian children in my social feed. Day after day, children. Living. Dead. Struggling. Fighting back. Children covered in dust with scarves over their mouths helping other Palestinians in Gaza try to save other Palestinians from the siege in Gaza. In the rubble.

This kind of feed I see in the days after the Al Aqsa attack of October 7 by Hamas and then the response by Israel. The response was supposed to be about Hamas and the safety of the Israeli people but then quickly accelerated into outright destruction and death. Some eventually call it genocide. As I write this, my friend, the poet Silvana Straw, writes that the number of dead children in Gaza is over 11,000. Is that all, I wonder? By the time of this publication, it is a lot more.

In my feed, buildings are collapsing, bombs exploding, bodies are pulled from piles and piles of rocks and dust. Teary-eyed men carry their sons and daughters, dead or injured, to hospitals which are also being bombed by Israel. This is Gaza, in real time, the largest prison on earth many call it. An abomination of humans on human evil. And all sanctioned by the United States, the country where I was born and where I live.

Yes, I am an American. I am African American but American. It is shameful to watch. Complicit? Yes, all Americans are complicit. How can we not be? So yes, I must dissent.

To be an American today as America continues to act as a world empire is to like living with Al Capone. Yes, Al Capone, the Chicago gangster of American criminal folklore. Al Capone does terrible things. He kills people. He rips people off. He takes from others by force. America, my country, does horrible things. America is Al Capone.

As for this struggle, it supports Israel and its killing of Palestinians unconditionally. It provides the guns and bombs for the killing. Al buys the silence of most Americans with endless coffee shops, streaming services, and food and beverage on every street corner in most of America's big and large cities. There is booze, legal weed shops, and electrical charge stations for fancy new electric cars. You live with Al Capone, the world's baddest gangster.

Gaza and the Palestinian people are oppressed and occupied because of the United States. Children are dying in Gaza because of my country. If America pulled back its support, the last 75 years of Palestinian history would have been different. I have little doubt. It does not have to be like it is.

In the early days of the invasion of Gaza, I remember predicting that things were going to be very bad for the ordinary Palestinian. Not because I am more adept than others at geopolitics but because I had seen this movie before. My prediction was simple: Hamas' attack into Israel on October 7 and the killing of many Israelis would justify almost any level of violence into Gaza. The U.S. would back it. Totally. I also knew that if any American wavered from the party line of America's ruling political class, they would be criticized for not supporting Israel unconditionally. As Noam Chomsky likes to say, consent would be manufactured. Dissent would be squashed.

Jewish-Americans who did not and do not support U.S. policy faced ferocious attacks from their own. Jewish friends of mine were called self-hating Jews for not supporting what was happening in Gaza to ordinary Palestinians who had suffered for decades under the occupation long before Hamas even existed.

I have long dissented from official U.S. policy regarding the Israel-Palestine conflict. The occupation. The settler colonialism. When I was a kid I never understood it. It was always explained to me as Arabs hating Jewish people. In 1972, when several Jewish athletes were kidnapped and eventually killed by Arab men in Munich, Germany, at the 1972 Olympics, everyone said this was about the hatred of Jewish people, that's all. What did I know?

Years later when I began to understand it better, I began to ask questions. Especially in 1983 after the suicide truck bombing of the U.S. Marine Barracks in Beirut. Why would someone do that? Then, in 1987, the First Intifada erupted, and I would see little Palestinian children on the news throwing rocks at tanks with no fear at all. They were prepared to die for their freedom.

Many years ago I was called "anti-Semitic" by a Jewish person I knew in passing. I had posted online that I thought the situation in Israel/Gaza/The West Bank regarding the Palestinian people was just like the Native Americans in the United States. It was classic settler colonialism and ethnic cleansing. What was the argument I asked?

I was dismissed back then. I was advised that this was different. The Palestinians were in the wrong. I didn't get it. I remember thinking at the time that it was time to study harder.

Why did little Palestinian boys risk death by throwing rocks at Israeli soldiers? Why did Israel shoot some of these children when they were throwing rocks? Why did Israel target journalists for reporting from Gaza? Why did people blow themselves up just to kill Israelis? Because they were evil?

So I spent years after that reading historians and academics who knew the history of the conflict. Israeli historians like Bennie Morris and the great Illan Pappé. And writers like the Palestinian scholar Edward Said and the Jewish dissident Norman Finklestein. Poets like Mahmoud Darwish. I also became friends with Palestinians, Jewish people, and others in America who knew the conflict. They all had lived in the region. Most live in either Israel or the West Bank. Some also had connections to Gaza. By the time I had spent years reading books, articles, and watching films on the conflict, I knew my instincts were correct.

This was settler colonialism. This was ethnic cleansing. Illan Pappé noted that it was always clear what Israel was over the years. "The idea that Zionism is settler colonialism is not new," Pappé said, "Palestinian scholars in the 1960s did not frame Israel as just a British colony or an American one but regarded it as a phenomenon that existed in other parts of the world—settler colonialism." The central feature of settler colonialism, according to Pappé, is the natives must be removed. The forced removal of 750,000 Palestinians by Israeli soldiers happened in 1948 (it is known historically as the 'Nakba'). The current siege of Gaza is another chapter in removal by the Zionist project.

In Palestinian writer Fida Jiryis' memoir, *Stranger in My Own Land*, Jiryis quotes Palestinian author Fawaz Turki's account of the Nakba (Turki was born in 1940 in Haifa):

> *These people have walked off with our home and homeland, with our moveable and immovable property, with our land, our farms, our shops, our public buildings, our paved roads, our cars, our theaters, our clubs, our parks, our furniture, our tricycles.*

According to Jiryis, the taking of Palestine and the displacement of the Palestinian people by force began under the British who had colonized Palestine after the fall of the Ottoman Empire. Jiryis writes that early on Jewish lawyers condemned the treatment of the Palestinian people as "legalized terror" and described the system the British imposed before the Nakba as "unprecedented in the civilized world."

But in 1948, the state of Israel was founded, and the Israeli people stepped into the place of the British full scale. Israel has never looked back. The Zionist project was launched. If you say what I just wrote in some circles today, you will get dismissed as anti-Semitic. Before and after the October 7 attack in Israel that led to the full-scale siege of Gaza, you could not even tell the truth about Palestine without receiving major pushback. If you advocate for Palestinian self-determination (or a separate Palestinian state) for the Palestinian people today many will call you anti-Semitic.

Up is down, right is left, water is not wet, and fire is not hot.

But African Americans, many, never bought this line. Uniformly across the board, Black people in America identified with the cause of the Palestinians. The struggle against colonial occupation and oppression, which historically we understood.

When the conflict first broke out, a few friends of mine were contacted by various Jewish leaders and asked why won't African Americans support the Jewish people and Israel right now? The implication beneath the overtures is that Jewish-Americans supported the cause of civil rights for Black Americans in the 20th century; don't we remember?

In fact, we do remember. The cause of civil rights for all Americans was/is righteous. The siege of Gaza and the oppression of the Palestinian people is a crime against humanity.

African Americans still do identify with the historic struggle of the Jewish people and condemn hate and anti-Semitism as much as we condemn racism. But what Israel is doing in Gaza to the Palestinians, with the approval of a lot of American Jews, is genocidal. The children who threw the rocks at Israeli tanks know what is happening to their people. The children who die each day in Gaza are prepared to die for what's right.

Plainly put, African Americans understand the quest for self-determination for the Palestinian people. Black America wants that as well. That is our goal as world citizens. The young people, Generation Z and younger, see that as well, and they are beginning to wage that never-ending struggle for that goal. Every day in my social media feed they are calling for change, standing with the Palestinian people and yelling "Free Palestine" just as I once yelled "Free South Africa" with my comrades over 30 years ago to end apartheid rule in South Africa.

As Gaza burned and crumbled, young African Americans all over America organized and joined protest marches calling for "Cease Fire" in Gaza. They organized poetry readings in support of the Palestinian people all around D.C., my city. They were joined by a multiethnic group of dissenters including young people from various backgrounds—Jewish, Palestinian, Arab-American, Asian, Latino, and other represented ethnic groups. They are the future of the struggle. They are pushing for different policies. They want a different world. They know the struggle must continue day by day, minute by minute, for equal justice, peace, and human rights in the world. They know, as we did, the meaning of a luta continua – "the struggle continues..."

Rafeek means "Comrade" in Arabic.

References

Jiryis, Fida. *Stranger in My Own Land.* Hurst and Company, 2022.

Pappé, Illan. *Ten Myths About Israel,* Verso, 2007.

Turki, Fawaz, "Reflections on the Nakba," *Journal of Palestine Studies*, Vol. 28 No. 1 (1998).

Whose Children? What Futures?
The Selective Vocabulary
of War and Peace

Julianne Malveaux

For a moment, the song was ubiquitous. Twenty-two-year-old Whitney Houston dropped her version of "The Greatest Love of All" in 1985. If you attended church, a children-focused event, or a Black-folk banquet, you heard it crooned. The lyrics speak to our idealized version of childhood, a version that only a minority of the world's children have the opportunity to experience.

> *I believe the children are our future*
> *Teach them well and let them lead the way*
> *Show them all the beauty they possess inside*
> *Give them a sense of pride to make it easier*
> *Let the children's laughter remind us how we used to be.*

The words, while uplifting, are inspirational, aspirational, and unequal. What children are we talking about? We were never talking about enslaved children, who started working almost as soon as they were born. To be sure they had moments of joy and laughter, but that laughter was eclipsed by the reality of their enslavement. Are we talking about children who worked so long and so hard that Congress first proposed legislation regulating the use of children in the workplace in 1906? Are we talking about migrant children who are being illegally used in the workplace? Are we considering the many states that would repeal federal child labor laws to allow the employment of children, even in dangerous conditions.

I believe that children are the future. We all buy into the idealized version of childhood, even as we acknowledge the unequal versions of idealized childhood. To remind us how we used to be. Each of us has precious memories of childhood, idealized or not. I always enjoy watching children playing, thinking of my own playtimes, watching the children's choir singing, studying their facial expressions to consider what kind of adults they might evolve into. The little girl who rises in the sanctuary to read that Sunday's scripture – will she be a leader, a thinker, a queen? What can I tell from the set of her shoulders, from the way she confidently tackles her task?

Gazan children are among those who will not have laughter. They are merely struggling to survive. Unfortunately, their childhood, their humanity, has been swallowed by the politics of the conflict in Israel. Let me insert the obligatory disclaimer. What Hamas did on October 7 was brutal and wrong. Let me also invoke context. Why did Hamas attack Israel on October 7, killing as many as 1,300 people and taking hostages? Why has Israel been grabbing land in Palestine, building settlements on land that did not belong to them? As wrong as Hamas was for their October 7 attack, reasonable people might consider the provocation.

About 1,300 Israelis lost their lives, people who were simply enjoying a music festival. In retaliation, the Israeli Defense Force (IDF) has massacred thousands. The Bible talks about an eye for an eye, but the Netanyahu interpretation is an eye for ten eyes, or maybe twenty or thirty, given the losses that have been documented. Hamas does not bear the burden of the Israeli aggression. Instead, innocent civilians, especially children, are the victims of Israel's out-of-order and out-of-control attacks. Israel's behavior has attracted international condemnation, and some of their staunchest allies have decried their awful effort. They say they will wipe out Hamas. What about the children?

According to an April 4 report from the international organization Save The Children, "Nearly 26,000 children---or just over two percent of Gaza's child population---have been killed or injured in Gaza in six months of a war which has decimated the health system and severed access to education." The report notes that while 33 children were killed in Israel, 13,800 have been killed in Gaza, and 12,009 have been injured. Additionally, 113 children have been killed in the West Bank, and 725 injured. Some will dispute these numbers, though they come from the UN Office for the Co-ordination of Humanitarian Affairs (OCHA) and the Ministry of Health in Gaza. UNICEF has reported that at least 1,000 children have had one or both legs amputated, and about 30 out of 36 hospitals have been bombed.

I believe that children are the future? Thousands of children have had their lives snuffed out, and thousands more have been impaired. As malnutrition and starvation increase, more will die, not because of military attacks, but because Israel is using food as a weapon of war. While the situation is constantly shifting, the many ways that Israel has prevented the transfer of food and other humanitarian supplies is unacceptable. The "accidental" targeting of World Central Kitchen convoys is a manifestation of Israel's inhumanity. World philanthropist José Andrés has provided nutritional assistance during many world food crises. They had clearance from the IDF to deliver food. Eight people who were bringing food to the hungry were massacred by Israel, which offered both a tepid and unprecedented apology for their callousness. Tepid—it was "inadvertent," as if the killing of thousands of children was unintended. Unprecedented—Israel does not apologize, but their tottering world reputation is on the line.

I contrast the notion of idyllic childhood with the images I see on my television screen. A CNN reporter interviewed a little girl, no more than eight years old. She lay on the ground, maybe on a blanket, looking wan and sounding tired and very sad. She is explaining to the reporter that she is hungry and thirsty. She just got half a bottle of water, and asked for the whole thing, but she was told there was not enough to go around. Her smudged round face and her thready voice are like a body blow to me. Will this girl survive? What does her future look like? How in good conscience can the world accept the starvation that is staring us down?

Another news image is of two middle-aged Israeli women blocking trucks bringing supplies to Gaza. They are passionate in their conviction that they will "starve" (the word they used) Gazans until the hostages are released. They have no notion that they are holding children hostage. They care about their children but not about other children. They would probably not relent if they saw the little Palestinian girl, laying on the ground, begging for more water. Which children's futures are we committed to? And what seeds are we sowing for future possibilities?

The horrors of the Holocaust sway world opinion in favor of Israel, and the United States has been Israel's most faithful ally. Our country gives at least $3.3 billion annually for military aid. We manufacture the weapons they use to kill and wound Palestinian children, and we hide behind the rhetoric that Israel has the right to exist. How many children's lives will be sacrificed on the altar of their flawed creation and flawed existence?

José Andrés, who lost workers and colleagues to Israel's unbridled aggression, described this war as "a war against humanity itself." "Humanitarians and civilians should never pay the consequences of war," Andrés explained in reaction to Israel's attacks of the World Central Kitchen convoy. Under Netanyahu's immoral leadership, Israel has embraced inhumanity, and civilians, especially children, have paid the price.

There is some evidence, reports the *Guardian*, that individual children have been shot without provocation by Israeli soldiers. Dr. Fozia Ali treated seven-or-eight-year-old children at a European public hospital in southern Gaza who had sniper shots to their brains. "They were not combatants, they were small children," she told the *Guardian*. Some doctors believe these children were deliberately targeted, and deliberately and callously shot. These children are not the "collateral damage" of bombs, airstrikes, or crumbling buildings. They were shot. IDF soldiers made a decision to shoot them. Some were holding the white flags of surrender and were shot anyway.

Little of this information seeps into the mainstream media. Instead, we are treated to photos of the hostages, to interviews with weeping women who want their sons and husbands home. I'd like also to see interviews with weeping Palestinian women who had to flee their homes with their children, losing their husbands and other relatives. Do we have equivalent compassion, or are we so eager to embrace Israel's victimhood that we ignore the other victims, those who shoulder a greater burden of loss?

There is no idyllic childhood for Gazan children. Instead of embracing the beauty they possess inside, they are struggling to simply survive. When I juxtapose the notion of idyllic childhood, of children running, playing, being, with the image of a small Palestinian girl, I am struck by the myopia that allows the IDF to target children. I am also repulsed by the ways the world, in embracing Israel, seems to signal that this is acceptable.

> *I believe the children are our future*
> *Teach them well and let them lead the way*
> *Show them all the beauty they possess inside*
> *Give them a sense of pride to make it easier*
> *Let the children's laughter remind us how we used to be.*

If we believe in the equivalency of humanity, if we believe that a life is a life, then we must embrace these broken Gazan children and condemn those who have targeted and attacked them. Many will say that any criticism of Israel is anti-Semitic. With the carnage that Israel has rained on Gazan children, criticism of Israel is humanitarian and appropriate. What about the children? Once we all were children. Now, too many children have no future, and our world is the loser because of Israel's inhumanity.

Genocide in Gaza—Save The Babies

Herb Boyd

On my fourth trip to Israel/Palestine in 2009 I was part of a peace delegation led by the Reverend Al Sharpton. As a reporter, I was there with the filmmaker Eddie Harris to document the journey. To capture more than the meetings between Yasser Arafat and other members of the Palestinian National Authority, Eddie and I ventured to parts of Gaza to gather scenes for our proposed documentary, which evolved into *Trek to the Holy Land.* One of the neighborhoods we fleetingly passed was Jabalya.

For several minutes we focused on the children playing in a field, kicking a soccer ball, and generally enjoying themselves. Like most children, once they noticed us, they were curious why two Black men were interested in their game. After a few words of Arabic with them, mostly greetings, we took our leave but filmed them from a distance. Those memories returned to me on Oct. 31, 2024, when the Israeli Defense Forces (IDF) targeted Jabalya and carried out one of the deadliest attacks in Gaza, killing 128 people, destroying some 30 buildings, and maiming countless Gazans. Since that tragedy, an example of genocidal atrocity, more than 26,000 Palestinians have been killed and 64,487 wounded according to the Gaza Health Ministry---and these numbers recorded at the end of January were sure to increase. The humanitarian crisis in Gaza has polarized American politics and communities at the same time that it has created global reactions, none more fervent than the one emanating from South Africa, which in its charge of genocide speaks with authority on the issue.

The IDF said the attack was precipitated because they were "targeting a military compound." Similar assertions and explanations have been given for the barrage of rockets in and around the Al-Ahli Arab Hospital in October, making it among the 22 hospitals that have been bombed or damaged. The purpose of these attacks, the IDF has repeatedly stated, was to root out the cadre and command leadership of Hamas. But this has often occurred without any regard for innocent civilians. If, for example, your house is infested with vermin, you don't bomb the house; you try to locate the nest for extermination.

Nothing was more distressing than to see videos of children caught in the throes of these battles. The depiction of their mutilated and decomposed bodies, many of them still in bed, was evidence of the total horror at one besieged hospital. It's good to know that UNICEF is moving forthrightly, providing them with water, food, and medical attention.

As UNICEF stated, "The cost to children and their communities of this violence will be borne out for generations to come."

In effect, the Hamas attack that is the source of the current war must be seen as another horrendous act in an ongoing fight in Israel/Palestine. Ellen Davidson in her insightful article on Portside.org captured the essence of this history and amplified Israel's apartheid-like governance of the territory. She wrote that "One of the central tenets of the South African system was dispossession from the land and control of resources by white settlers. Israel has replicated this process. In Israel/Palestine, the land that is nominally under Palestinian control constitutes 22% of historic Palestine. Hundreds of thousands of Palestinians were made permanent exiles in 1947–48, as Zionist militias terrorized and massacred whole villages. Many more were forced out by the invasion in 1967 when the Israeli army took over the West Bank and Gaza in an occupation that continues to this day."

Davidson then itemizes how the constrictions of apartheid have prevailed in the nation-state of the Jewish people. Palestinian refugees who were born here are not allowed to return and claim citizenship, she cited. A wall bifurcating the districts cuts them off from freedom of movement; those who reside in the Occupied Territories risk being detained for six months; in the West Bank, Palestinians are subject to the control of the military, much in the manner Black Africans were accosted and arrested in South Africa. These are the kinds of constraints that have severely limited the opportunities for Palestinians to exercise their civil and human rights. Eddie and I encountered some of this during our visit when we sought to visit the Temple Mount. We were never told why we weren't allowed to enter, but after they asked us to speak opening passages of the Qur'an, which I did, the armed guard still prohibited us from entering. Later, I learned that all Muslims over 45 and women over 35 were not allowed to enter at that time.

Among the various measures to stem the conflict, the UN's highest court stated on January 26 that "Israel must ensure its forces do not commit genocide against Palestinians in Gaza." This charge of genocide was initiated by South Africa, and it delivered a blow to Israel, and it put pressure on the U.S. and other Israeli allies. Under the 1948 Genocide Convention, Palestinians are a protected group and the court's president, Joan E. Donoghue, observed in the Hague, that the war against "Hamas is causing massive civilian casualties, extensive destruction of civilian infrastructure and the displacement of the overwhelming majority of the population of Gaza."

The ruling from the International Court of Justice was met with approval by pro-Palestinian supporters outside the Hague, where they waved flags and chanted "Ceasefire Now" and "Free, Free Palestine!" The response from Israel's security minister, Itamar Ben-Gvir, came via a tweet: "Hague Schmague."

A ruling from the court does not guarantee that any of its demands will be met; curtailing the assaults from the IDF will not be halted by a decree from any court. The feud between the Arabs and Jews is reminiscent of the fight between the Hatfields and the McCoys, although, in the Middle East, this is genealogically a battle between cousins. More important to us here in the U.S., and this is not to diminish the global implications, is how we resolve our differences. And in many respects, they are as daunting as the international ones.

Our great prophet and seer, Dr. Martin Luther King, Jr., who often had Jews in his cadre, many of whom marched with him, rebuked the notion of Black anti-Semitism and pointed out in a *Playboy* interview in 1965, "Need I remind anyone of the awful beating suffered by Rabbi Arthur Lelyveld of Cleveland when he joined the civil rights workers there in Hattiesburg, Mississippi? And who can ever forget the sacrifice of two Jewish lives, Andrew Goodman and Michael Schwerner, in the swamps of Mississippi? It would be impossible to record the contribution that the Jewish people have made toward the Negro's struggle for freedom--and it has been great." It is perhaps based on this long association that many older Black Americans and organizations sympathize with Jews, especially after the horrific attack in October. For many of the younger members of their families and community, their marches with Black Lives Matter and other groups in support of the Palestinians are mainly a result of their identification with the current plight of Palestinians in Gaza, something far more immediate than the injustices experienced by Jews. Dr. King also cited the old law about an eye for an eye leaving everybody blind. But the blind and eyeless in Gaza will be mostly Palestinians.

As we have learned over the years about American history and policies, the international agenda is inextricably tied to domestic policies, and the conflict in the Middle East reminds us again of a fresh inflection point, and we hope a positive resolution is forthcoming, especially for the helpless children who know nothing of the fury and madness that endangers their existence.

All the lives in Gaza are precious, but as Marvin Gaye reminded us many years ago, if you truly love you got to save the children. Save the babies.

Confronting Dehumanization: Palestinian Youth and the Leviathan of Zionism and Western Imperialism

Jason Cohen

How is it that videos, photos, and stories circulate daily on social media platforms that brutally show Palestinian children starving, mourning, covered in rubble, or deceased due to Israeli military and institutional actions, yet seconds later local and national news stations will run segments glorifying and justifying Israeli actions in the name of "fighting terrorism" and "self-defense?" What we are witnessing in real-time is an orchestrated maneuver by the Euro-American bourgeoisie along with their allies within the media establishments to deal with a growing legitimacy crisis faced by the institution of liberal democracy. Historically, liberal democracy and the market economy have been portrayed as the most enlightened and humane form of societal organization, so much so that various ideologies were developed ranging from manifest destiny, mission civilisatrice, and Zionism which held that it was one's duty to spread Euro-American modernity to the "underdeveloped, barbarian or oriental" world. These discourses that are fundamental to the hegemonic powers have been completely destabilized in the past few years due to continued struggles by the African diaspora against police terrorism in the United States and Europe, the necropolitical response by Western governments toward the COVID-19 pandemic, and the ongoing genocide in Palestine. Each of these situations has destabilized the notion that Western governments and the political systems they manage valorize the human subject. Contrary to claims of the universality of the human within the liberal democratic paradigm, it is stunningly clear, especially in the case of Palestinians, that in a world system embedded within the structures of racial capitalism and settler colonialism, the ontological nature of the human is inherently circumscribed.

The task before us now is to uncover the endogenous and exogenous dynamics that have allowed Israel to continue its settler-colonialist plans in historical Palestine with the firm support of Western imperialist powers. We must recognize that the current genocidal campaign against Gazans is just one event within a centuries-long process of Israeli settler colonization. Denoting the current crisis is not meant to de-emphasize the severity and human loss in Gaza since October 8, 2023. Instead, it is meant to historically situate the contemporary to understand how multifarious dynamics and societal structures have provided a basis for this genocidal campaign to unfold with unwavering international support in the West. I have identified three frames that are needed to understand the current situation, they are political-economic, geopolitics, and ideological. Each of these frameworks is not disparate but integrally connected as events and processes play out in reality. Before delving into a terse analysis using these frameworks I want to proffer a remark on methodology. Within the various historiographies pertaining both to Palestine and critical analysis of social structures of various capitalist societies such as Apartheid South Africa, there has been a tense debate surrounding the efficacy of a Marxist methodology in explaining the developments in these polities. Edward Said in his work on Orientalism and Robert Fatton in his analysis of Black Consciousness in Apartheid South Africa have both criticized Marxist analyses due to the "economistic" nature of the literature and claim that a major caveat is found within the "base-superstructure" method due to the prominence of the economic base in this analysis. Thus, they argue that there is a dearth of focus on civil society and ideology in such analyses which label these aspects of the superstructure as "epiphenomenons." As a Marxist, I have contemplated these criticisms, and although I do not necessarily believe they are completely correct, they remain omnipresent as I develop my analysis and, guided by the new discipline of racial capitalism, aim to show how a Marxist analysis of Israeli settler colonialism can elucidate the relational dynamics between superstructural phenomenon such as ideologies, epitomized in Zionism and orientalism in our case, alongside the political economic dynamics inherent in colonization and capitalist development.

When discussing the "birth" of Israel we must harken back to the era in which Euro-American imperialism reached its zenith. Thus, we find ourselves in the late 19th century, a period characterized by various diplomatic meetings of European nations as they sought to rearticulate the maps and boundaries of the "uncivilized" and "unclaimed" world, namely Africa and Asia, and solidify European imperial expansion. Contemporaneously, the United States and Canada in the late 19th century were undergoing a series of military campaigns that were intertwined with settler projects "from below" to completely extinguish the numerous Indigenous nations that were seen as obstacles to the "God-ordained" processes of expansion across the entire continent of North America. Therefore, during this era, we recognize that the two main forms of colonization, classical colonialism and settler colonialism, were integral to the expansion and construction of the Euro-American empire and individual national construction projects. Although each type of colonialism focused on the exploitation of distinct parts of the colonies with classical colonialism focusing on proletarianizing the colonial

Indigenous while settler colonialism dealt with the appropriation of land for the settler state, there was/is a commonality in the ideological and cultural discourses that developed as imperial projects expanded. Regarding Euro-American attitudes towards the claims to humanity by the colonized, cultural productions that were integrated with the racialist ideologies rampant in the Euro-American imaginary were necessary in justifying the various bloody, genocidal, and expansionist colonialist projects. As Edward Said remarks, "Theses of Oriental backwardness, degeneracy, and inequality with the West most easily associated themselves early in the nineteenth century with ideas about the biological bases of racial inequality." Although in this case, Said is only referring to works that deal with the "Near East," there have been numerous academic works that have discussed the role of cultural productions in justifying empire and legitimizing racial discrimination/exclusion within the United States, Australia, and other nations.

So where does Israel fit into this excursion into imperial history? Well, in this era of high imperialism and the various transnational ideological, racial, and cultural discourses, the notion of a Jewish national project developed. We must remember that this was not only a period of imperial construction, but also a period of national construction and liberation in Europe. Thus, various Jewish intelligentsia sought to grapple with the dismal climate of European anti-Semitism and constructed a Jewish "national liberation" project via the settler colonization of Jews in an undetermined area. As Laura Robson points out, Zionists were not entirely united on the exact location where the future Jewish settler colony would be as there were disagreements surrounding the efficacy of Palestine as a suitable area in the short term, thus bringing to exist settlement schemes in Uganda and throughout Latin America. Zionists ultimately adopted many discourses that were imbued in Orientalism and sought to obtain imperial sponsors to jump-start this settler colonial project of "national liberation." As we know, it was the British who obliged and steered the path to Israeli settler colonial development once it obtained the Palestinian mandate after the First World War. From the 1920s until 1948, Zionist settlers migrated to mandatory Palestine in migratory waves known as "Aliyah" and developed the political and economic basis for the mass dispossession of Palestinians during this period and drastically in the Nakba in 1948, the ethnic cleansing that accompanied Israel's "independence."

Israel's post-1948 history is integral for two main reasons. First, we can see how Israel became "a beachhead in the Middle East" for the Euro-American imperialists as Stephen Gowan has accurately described this garrison state. Secondly, it is in this period, extending to contemporary times, in which we can begin discussing the dehumanization of Palestinian youth and the multifarious discourses that were produced by the Zionist establishment to justify this abject dehumanization of the whole Palestinian people. Now these processes may seem disparate but are entangled within the endogenous and exogenous development of Israel within the world system. The main policies of Israeli political development I want to focus on in this section are those that deal with the so-called "demographic question." Even with the massive ethnic cleansing during the Nakba in 1948, Israeli settlers and the political authorities remained anxious because a sizeable Palestinian population remained within the territorial boundaries of Israel. As Lorenzo Veracini makes clear, one of the most dangerous things to a settler colonial polity is the continued presence of actual Indigenous people within the territorial boundaries. This is because settler colonial mythos relies on the notion that the settler is the only ontological subject that is Indigenous to the territory. Secondly, the presence of an Indigenous community means that the "national question" is never fully put to rest; thus, as Rouhana and Sabbagh-Khoury explain, Israel turned to the militarization of Palestinian life and counter-insurgency techniques to stamp out any inkling of resistance within Israel and later in the occupied territories. This process of securitization via militarization and counterinsurgency is integral to both the continued dehumanization of Palestinians to this day and Israel's role within the world system. Before we proceed to the main discussion regarding dehumanization, we will take one look at the foreign role Israel played. Israel remained a "bulwark of Western civilization" in the Middle East during the era of Pan-Arabism and the so-called Soviet threat, which combined fueled the development of a vast Euro-American military apparatus as epitomized by CENTCOM. In the face of a growing anti-colonial tide in the Middle East and worldwide as we shall see, Israel became a major player in preventing the rise of progressive governments who sought to break free from both colonialism and the hegemonic neocolonial order. One only has to remember that Israel at one point occupied the Sinai Peninsula and continues to occupy the Golan Heights and constantly conducts air strikes against Syrian civilian and military infrastructure to this day. In addition, Israel was and remains a major exporter of counterinsurgency, military and surveillance techniques, and apparatuses, and provided aid to Apartheid South Africa and numerous Latin American nations such as El Salvador and Mexico, both nations that adopted genocidal techniques as counterinsurgency against Indigenous liberation movements. Although this is a very vague description of Israel's role in US foreign policy, I believe it is enough to recognize how the inhumanity of Israeli tactics against Palestinians have become internationalized not only due to Israel, but this state plays a great role in this process of maintaining capitalist hegemony via genocidal tactics that are cloaked within the discursive context of counter-insurgency.

Finally, we can circle back to the conversation regarding the dehumanization of Palestinians and the connection to the circumscribed nature of what it means to be ontologically human within the world capitalist order and settler colonialism. Overall, I have sought to elucidate the general history of Zionist settler colonialism, providing an idea of the historical contingency of Zionism and its genocidal project. Now, since this anthology aims to focus upon the Palestinian youth who are forced to deal with the Israeli system of dehumanization, we will be able to explore how Zionism as an ideology and the construction of the militarized security apparatus truly impacts Palestinians day to day, through the lens of the youth. I joined this important project because of the precarious position of Palestinian youth whether they are located within the territorial boundaries of Israel, within Gaza, West Bank, or the diaspora. We will get back to the discourse and mechanisms of Israeli securitization, but for a moment we should contemplate what it means for a child, teenager, and young adult to be brought up under a societal order in which their everyday lives are characterized by precarity, criminalization, and the existential threat of personal or familial death. We must ask why such a horrid anti-human regime of occupation, securitization, and militarization is utilized to structure the lives of youth in Palestine. Why is one of the most vulnerable sections of the Palestinian population targeted and dehumanized so virulently by the Israeli state and settlers?

As an adjunct to the empirical evidence of the dehumanization of Palestinian youth, I wish to discuss an anecdotal experience of mine as I walked to Dag Hammarskjold Plaza for a rally that combined climate justice and Palestinian liberation. On this day I wore my keffiyeh in solidarity with my Palestinian comrades and was called over by a man who was inquisitive about my relationship to the Palestinian cause. After I let him know that I was Jewish, he went on a tangent in which he claimed that he was a former member of the IOF (Israeli Occupation Force) and sought to convince me that I was making a huge mistake against the Jews and God. Honestly, nothing out of the ordinary in encounters with Zionists. Before I left, he told me something that has not left my mind ever since. As he motioned his hands making the figure of an adult and a child, he told me, "No matter what, they are all terrorists, as simple as that." This anecdote I believe is exemplary in elucidating one of numerous subjectivities that the policies of securitization of Palestinian communities within Israel and the Occupied Territories combined with religious Zionist ideology could produce. The interface between structural processes within Israel and the development of Israeli identity is integral to better understanding the reproduction of the settler colonial project and what this reproduction means for the subaltern, in this case, Palestinians. As we can see from the anecdote, the settler colonial mythos and dehumanization of Palestinians were actively integrated into my interlocutor's identity. This experience and the development of an Israeli settler colonial identity remind me of the concept of "colonial inhabitation" as proffered by Malcolm Ferdinand in his recent work *Decolonial Ecology*. He argues that "colonial inhabitation" is a philosophical and ontological condition that requires "othercide" or the extermination or full dehumanization of the "other," and also consists of a complete reorientation of the social relations within the colony, not just between "humans" and "property" but also through the construction of exploitative relations between the *colon* and the environment. Although Ferdinand was discussing the colonial context of the French Caribbean instead of a purely settler colonial context, I believe the conceptual formation of "colonial inhabitation" will be useful in elucidating the ontological nature of the Israeli settler colonist.

Some readers may wonder why I am so focused on investigating the Israeli settler when discussing the dehumanization of Palestinian youth and may rightfully argue that I am decentering Palestinian youth at this moment. In my view, we cannot utterly understand the dehumanization of Palestinian youth and Palestinians at large without understanding the Israeli settler, who is an active agent of the settler colonial project. The ramifications for such a claim are important when discussing the brutalization and murder of Palestinians in the West Bank and when confronting hegemonic discourses surrounding the "civilian Israeli" and the always "terrorist or barbarian" Palestinian. This discourse is extremely powerful even within supposed progressive circles and it serves to naturalize the Israeli settler colonial project and obscures the dynamics that underpin the social formation of settler colonialism itself. Without understanding the dynamics of specific social formations, the subalterns are unable to understand the nature of their oppression and discover the contradictions within the social formation. Without discussing this second facet of the agency of the Israeli settler vis-à-vis their role in expanding and solidifying the structural basis of settler colonialism, I believe we will never actually construct a solidarity with the Palestinians that is based in material reality; instead, it will be a half-hearted solidarity that continues to rely on liberal-democratic values that are racialized themselves.

Now, we will pivot back to Zionist settler colonists' agency and their orientation toward Palestinian youth. Once again, I will provide an anecdote that was instructive for me in understanding the vile nature of Zionism as an ideology and the implicit discourse of Palestinian dehumanization. A couple of years ago I joined a counter-protest of the Israeli "independence day" parade in New York City. There was no doubt in my mind that we would be witnesses to vitriolic and racist verbal and possibly, physical attacks, which we were as the police were motionless. At one point, I held a sign that focused on the Nakba, the brutal ethnic cleansing of Palestinians and the urbicidal destruction that wiped away any semblance that Palestinians might have lived in certain areas---an extremely violent event demographically and spatially for Palestinians. An older man who was walking with a Yeshiva class came up to me and said, "I'm glad the Nakba happened and was happy that it was occurring again," referring the Israeli airstrikes on Gaza and the continued settler colonization of the West Bank. Once again, the blatant nature of this encounter left me stunned, but meditating on this encounter provided greater evidence for the role that educational institutions were integral to the reproduction of social systems and ideologies, in this case, Zionism and Israel. Gramsci and Althusser are instructive here. The former discussed the role civil society plays in maintaining and instilling hegemonic ideas/systems, and the latter wrote the necessity of ideological reproduction for certain states and social formations to be reproduced and remain unchallenged. For our discussion surrounding Israeli settler or just Zionist agency, this encounter is extremely important because obviously in this case the teacher was not just reproducing knowledge embedded within the Zionist mythos passively but seemed to take immense pride in the fact of the Nakba and the continuing suffering of the Palestinian people. Yet again we see the active part played by settlers or Zionists in replicating and legitimizing the settler colonial project. We should meditate on this reality and once again remember that these are the valued subjects of bourgeois humanity, not the Palestinian, Congolese, or Sudanese child starving due to conditions created by imperialism.

In discussing this interface between state-led agents of settler colonization and the "grassroots settler movements" that are integral to any settler colonial project, we come back now to their orientation toward Palestinian youth. As mentioned earlier, Palestinian youth are labeled as a security threat, constantly living precarious lives either due to the economic de-development of Gaza, as Sara Roy has discussed at length, or the existential risk of being shot and detained by the IOF and settlers in the West Bank and within the territorial boundary of Israel proper. It should be clear to anybody that in the context of the current genocidal campaign against Gaza and Rafah, the Israeli state and its military apparatus do not have one ounce of care for Palestinian youth or Palestinians overall. Increasingly, the cynical declarations of Euro-American representatives of the bourgeoisie sound hollow when they claim that they are telling Netanyahu to "take precautions" in preventing the deaths of Palestinian civilians during bombing campaigns. Both the Israeli establishment and their imperial sponsors in the West have made it quite clear that Palestinians of all ages are not human enough to necessitate the cessation of bombing civilian areas, nor are they human enough to require a real transformation in humanitarian aid policy and in the policy of Israel refusing to allow fresh water into the Gaza Strip or Rafah.

What more can be said in the face of this blight on humanity? Over 30,000 lives were destroyed by the terroristic campaigns of the Israeli government, not to mention the lives lost in the pogroms throughout the West Bank during this period. For me, the goal of the Israeli government is clear; they desire to ethnically cleanse the Gaza Strip completely. They remember the Nakba of 1948 and have remodified their plans to ensure that the ethnic cleansing that began October 8, 2023, leaves no Palestinian within the Gaza strip, thus preventing a "security dilemma" when Israel chooses to annex Gaza completely. They target youth in this context to decimate any chance of the reproduction of Palestinians within Gaza. Whether by blatant military action or the state and settlers choosing to prevent necessary food and water into Rafah, the settler colonialists are committed to preventing the reproduction of Palestinians in Gaza. Indeed, these are gloomy and horrible times, but this tactic of the Zionists targeting the youth implicitly shows the power of this section of Palestinian society. The Israelis know that it is the youth who through their experiences with the oppressive Zionist entity develop a revolutionary subjectivity that is then nurtured by the heroic history of Palestinians and their cultural productions which serve as consciousness-raising mediums. It will be the youth who will fill the ranks of the Palestinian resistance shortly; it will be the Palestinian youth who ultimately launch the final intifada that will lead to the destruction of the Zionist entity and the new beginning of Palestinian, subaltern humanity, and national rebirth within historical Palestine. From the Jordan River to the Mediterranean Sea, olive groves will flourish, towns and villages will be rebuilt, and Palestinians will be able to enter Al-Aqsa without the threat of tear gassing by occupation forces.

There is no doubt in my mind that the Palestinian people will triumph and will not just free themselves but light a fire that tumbles neocolonialism throughout the Middle East and bring the Euro-American imperialist powers to their knees.

Acknowledgment

I want to thank Herb Boyd for helping me join this necessary anthology, along with all the other authors whose work will enter conversation with this piece. I also want to dedicate this article to my friend and my brother Adnan. May you and your family be able to go back to your home in Palestine, free from Zionism, free from terror, and full of peace, justice, and prosperity.

The Weapon of Truth
Molefi Kete Asante

When the African abolitionist Harriet Tubman helped deliver nearly 700 Africans to freedom during the Civil War, our chroniclers called her a master of the freedom train. She operated out of an intense sense of rightness that originated in the earliest cultures of African people. It is the same spirit that motivated Nelson Mandela and the South African liberators who knew that all forms of oppression are invitations to rebellion. In this brief essay, I assert the ethical value that invigorates the best tradition of African Americans as essential for a proper interpretation of the Israeli-Palestinian Conflict. That value, as I see it, is truth. Nothing escapes the door of truth. One cannot ever make a proper judgment or cast a decent vote based on untruth.

Truth is the easiest value to lose during conflict, but it is the only weapon in political crisis to help humans solve problems. To use the weapon of truth demands courage, bravery, and uprightness. This means that we cannot make false assumptions or refuse to confront our worst fears. Without truth we create mistakes that take us away from being human.

It is a mistake to assume that the Israeli-Palestinian War of 2023-2024 began on October 7, 2023. This is an untruth that cannot be accepted as the starting point of the conflict between the Israeli government and Palestinians. If it is accepted, it is a denial of the decades of oppression of Palestinians that have existed since the Nakba. Truth must not be sacrificed in the search for political advantage. As the ancient African sages from the time of Imhotep to Ogotomeli of the Dogon knew, the only path to holding back chaos is understanding the value of truth. Flashes of it during storms of falsehoods can only be considered half-truths and those flashes do not count in the battle against chaos.

The position I hold is derived from the principles of African ideas of *iwa rere*, good character, and *nefer*, goodness. Both these characteristics have been essential to making rational sense of the world. There is no dissembling or deception intended in telling the truth. Goodness, *nefer*, is both beautiful and correct, and the teller of the truth confronts all dissimulations. At this point we stand on the edge of understanding the crisis in the Israeli-Palestinian issue because we peel away the covering given to those who claim Hamas is the problem. If the October 7 killings and kidnappings had occurred in the West Bank, it would have been said that the problem was the Palestinian Authority. The truth is that Israel's war is against the Palestinian people, not Hamas. The more the Palestinian people are bombed and killed in revenge the more Hamas becomes the synonym for Palestinians in Gaza.

Two people encounter each other, one with a long history of rejection, pogroms, and the Holocaust; the other with a foreboding of events to come after the *Nakba* of 1948. In the dispossession and displacement of the Palestinians one sees the *asili*, seed, of October 7. It is not necessary in this essay to recall the various struggles, battles, wars, and *intifadas* that have beset the nation of Israel and the Palestinian people. But truth must be told to make sense, to understand, the violence that rains on the people of the area.

I am among the first to understand the horrific nature of the surprise attack on Israelis by the Hamas cadre of fighters who sought to assert their freedom by attacking many Israelis, some quite innocent, and others, soldiers of the Israeli Defense Force. It is a mistake to assume that the Palestinian killers of innocent Israelis are worse morally than the Israeli killers of innocent Palestinians.

All ethical traditions give oppressed people the right, indeed the obligation, to throw off their oppressors. One does not have to look in difficult places to discover the words of Israeli leaders about Hamas. One can also find harsh words from Hamas leaders about Israeli people. Yet it is truth that no amount of maiming and killing of children, women, and men in Gaza will bring about satisfaction to those who seek only revenge.

Reflecting on my own African ethical tradition, I think we must dismantle the idea of people who are different by religion and phenotypes and think more carefully about culture. A Jew and an Arab can have similar cultural beliefs about moral issues. But they are often confronted with different interpretations of the same history out of which emerges distinct conceptions and perceptions of political realities.

Humans can create infinite reasons for their actions, but we must understand that all excuses for doing something are not rational. Yet, to me, as a member of a people who were stolen, transported, enslaved, brutalized, and discriminated against, I feel the pain of all oppressed people who seek liberty. While the murder of 1,400 Israeli civilians is a disgrace to humanity, so, too, is the killing of nearly 40,000 or more innocents in Gaza. The endless rhetoric of blame, and the endless lack of grace that defies our best moral instincts, can catapult us into a frenzied world where military might makes lawlessness a code of a new humanity. It is that threshold that we must not cross, for if we do, we will barrel down a dystopian and dangerous place from which humanity may not soon recover.

As an Africologist, I am drawn to examples in African American history. In 1831, under brutal enslavement, Nat Turner rose up and killed his slaveowner and scores of others. The response of the white Virginia community was like the Israeli government's response to Hamas's attacks in Israel, the killing of over four hundred innocent Africans who had no part in Turner's rebellion. The white response to Nat Turner was out of all proportion to the 62 white deaths. A violent anger, nearly unhinged, captured the white population and led to an unequal and asymmetrical reaction that was seen as the slaughter of innocents. Ordinary Africans carrying out their duties as enslaved people, chopping down trees, washing clothes, cooking, and cleaning houses, were summarily taken and killed. Nat Turner was not simply hanged; he was beheaded, and his head preserved at a college in Ohio. Revenge killings took place in Virginia over several months. Whites felt that their security had been threatened by the boldness of Turner and those aligned with him. They felt that they had to re-assert their authority over the "lesser" beings to restore a sense of invulnerability to whites. Further, they wanted to assure themselves that no African person would ever think of revolting against oppression again. Yet between 1831 and 1860, the extent of black revolts, escapes, and resistance to enslavement soared as others rose up to demand their humanity. The truth is that it is human to resist oppression.

Clearly, the October 7, 2023, Hamas attack on Israeli civilians was violent and must be condemned by all humans who seek peaceful solutions to conflicts. Nevertheless, the Israeli government cannot get a pass to starve, freeze, or bomb innocent Palestinians and call that justice or the road to peace.

A concept that undergirds African cultural beliefs from ancient times is *Maat*. The early Nile Valley Africans believed that *Maat* was at the center of holding back chaos. The assertion of *Maat* is ongoing in our lives, to keep humans free of vile and violence, underscoring that if we live *Maat*, do *Maat*, and respect *Maat*, we will have a chance at peace. What is *Maat*? It is the constant search for what the philosopher Maulana Karenga calls justice, truth, righteousness, order, harmony, balance, and reciprocity.

Following the fundamental principles of *Maat, nefer*, and *iwa rere*, will convey us to the conclusion that a solution for conflict based in truth is possible. The two-state solution must be given a chance. One cannot speak of democracy in a polity where only one group, class, ethnic, or religious community has the right to decide for all the people. Yet it should be the objective of most people who love peace to find a solution that will give both people security and respect. This can never be done while one people seeks to dominate another. So why would the Israeli Netanyahu government not commit to a two-state solution?

Children are dying and suffering in Palestine. They are our children because we are human and no human who accepts human dignity can abandon the children of Gaza. They lack clean water, food, medical care, and parental protection. Gaza is an open wound on the conscience of the world. As much as any other massacre in modern times the attack on Gaza stands for unmitigated misery.

The Right-Wing Israel government has refused to allow some food to the people in Gaza. This is a war crime because now children are starving to death. How could any of us think that the right of Israel to defend itself means the starving of children in Gaza? Prime Minister Netanyahu and others in the government said at the beginning of the destruction of Gaza that they wanted to withhold food, water, and electricity. Is this in the interest of the dignity of Israelis? Palestinians?

I grew up in an era when Jews, like African Americans, held the high ground of ethical behavior for the struggle against white supremacy and the battle against the Nazi holocaust. Jewish leaders saw in the African American Struggle for Civil Rights a powerful ethic against domination, oppression, and brutality. Out of a common vision, Civil Rights leaders and Jewish progressives forged a front against discrimination and white racial supremacy and anti-Semitism. With the brutal assault on Gaza after the October 7, 2023, attack on innocent Israelis, the Israeli Defense Force managed to change the calculus of Jewish particularism by advancing on a ruthless revenge-filled drive to eradicate Gaza as a livable community. The place of Jews as persecuted people willing to defend other persecuted people dissolved during violence so egregious that one had to ask if the IDF had now become the Gestapo of the 21st century. Why would those who have suffered so severely from hatred now retaliate as if their foes are not humans? This is the puzzle to the response to October 7, 2023, which was a gruesome date but certainly not the only horrible date witnessed by the people of that region. To be against the wanton brutality of the Israeli government must not be confused with anti-Semitism. Africans have learned that nothing human can be placed outside of human possibilities. But we know that the ability to harness the most destructive tendencies in our minds is the only way to advance safety and security for everyone.

Truth rushes in where dishonor hides. It is truth that exposes the weaknesses of any argument that insists that violence is the way forward. The killing of innocent Palestinians is not atonement for the killing of innocent Jews; it is mutual violence, horrendous in thought and practice, which leads ultimately to the annihilation of both people.

What is a democratic government? Who would have the courage to declare that another solution, other than a two-state solution, is a true democratic solution based on protected rights under a new constitution for all the people of Israel and Palestine? If Israel now rejects a two-state solution, then why should not the world call for a truly democratic state that would see Jews and Arabs in the same state with equality? To be true, this is not the pattern in many Southwest Asian nations, but it is a radical solution in a democratic way. There is talk about democracy, but then what is the meaning of a democratic state? In my opinion, no one-god religious nation can be fully democratic, especially if they reduce those who do not accept their deity to a second-class position. Thus, for me, based on African ethical values, neither the idea of an Islamic State nor a Jewish State can be called democratic where such states inherently reject equality and equity for all people regardless of religion. Nevertheless, without a two-state solution to the crisis in Southwest Asia, the world may have to think about an authentic democracy.

The weapon of truth is a provocative instrument in the middle of confusion, blaming, Islamophobia, anti-Semitism, and anti-Africanism. With truth, we can restore our commitment to humanity, where humanity is valued and recognized and that of innocent Palestinians and innocent Israelis are not seen as of lesser value. Saving the Palestinians today must be seen to be as valuable as saving Israeli hostages. The hard truth is that we cannot defend the mass killing of Palestinians as we could never rejoice in the murder of innocent Israelis. Long live truth!

The Inhumane Situation in Gaza:
A Commentary
Edmund W. Gordon

We, inhabitants of the planet Earth, and especially those of us who are citizens of the United States of America, cannot be judged harshly enough by all the Gods of justice and humanity considering the situation we have permitted to occur and even enabled in the Middle Eastern Region of the world. The abuse and genocide against the Palestinian People is criminally sinful!

First, our nation, the USA, imposed a Jewish Nation on an unwilling Arab community of nations, albeit out of consideration for the protection of the humanity of the historically and unjustly abused Jewish peoples. To create a geographical home for the Jewish nation was a noble action! But we failed to negotiate a protected welcome for this alien, abused, and unwelcome People. And in support of their self-assertion, we armed this imposed group, more heavily than their neighbors, and basically against them. It is difficult to see humanness in this duplicitous benevolence. As if these infractions were not bad enough, the imposition of this "new" old nation on a defenseless Middle Eastern community was achieved at the price of the subordination - threatened elimination - of a weaker Palestinian nation. And now we stand by, wringing our hands, Neville Chamberlain-like, in assumed helplessness, as our Israeli, international protégées commit virtual genocide against their unwilling hosts. The Gods of Justice and Right cannot be smiling! The justice-loving peoples of the world should not be permitting this to happen. What we have fermented and are permitting to happen in the Middle East is poor foreign policy for the USA. It projects terrible international relations. It borders on our open endorsement and sponsorship of criminal behavior, especially because it seems to be motivated by domestic political pandering.

I am a developmental psychologist and educator. From my professional perspective, my country is committing an educational and criminal error, and I must say so as loudly and forthrightly as I can. Here we are tolerating and actively supporting the creation of conditions under which it is impossible for healthy child development to occur in Palestine. We are setting an evil and sinful example of acceptable national behavior for our children to follow. AND WE CANNOT CLAIM THAT WE DO NOT KNOW WHAT WE ARE DOING! We are aware of the possible negative consequences for the human development of the abused as well as the perpetrators. Nothing good can come of this situation in Gaza and Israel.

Not even for the survival of Israel! HOW CAN WE HOPE FOR THE STATE OF ISRAEL TO BE WELCOME IN THAT REGION OF THE WORLD, GIVEN ITS GENOCIDE AGAINST PALESTINE? Is Israel to survive at the price of the cost of the destruction of Palestine, and the distortion of the future development of its children? And we should not be unmindful of the toll such state-supported criminal behavior must be taking on the children of Israel. Not alone are they being taught to fear and hate the Palestinians, think of what they must be learning about human responsibility for the conditions of life and the protection of the very lives of other human beings.

I am also mindful of the plight of and impact on the USA and its members. The history of our nation is already morally stained by the history of our near genocide against the Native American and African American peoples. Our self-claimed glory is diminished by that history, not to mention our continuing responsibility for the underdevelopment of both of these discriminated against and subordinated peoples.

No matter how great the USA and Israel become, these histories of growth and survival at the price of genocidal abuse against weaker peoples will be a stain on our and Israel's existence and will have a stunting influence on the moral development of our victims and ourselves. What a price to have paid for even the survival and the thrival of Israel as a nation. Beyond the abuse and harm, what we have inflicted on other peoples is the shame and immorality we have brought onto ourselves. What moral negativity we have brought onto ourselves? The Scriptures say responsibility for the sins of the fathers falls on to the generations of them that follow.

Our financial, military, and moral support of what Israel is doing to the Palestinian people in Gaza is more than wrong. It is criminal on the parts of Israel and of us, US citizens. The blood on our hands is more obvious and it smells. It is evil and, to my Buddhist and Christian belief systems, it is sinful. I cannot stand by and watch in silence! The Gods will damn such sinful acts.

L'Dor V'Dor:
Our Sacred Obligation
to Generational Time
Rabbi Alissa Wise

A foundational obligation of Jewish adults is to pass on our traditions *l'dor v'dor*, from generation to generation. This stems from the idea that all the generations were present and part of the covenant God made with the newly liberated Israelites.

In the book of Deuteronomy, after the Israelites escaped bondage under a cruel Pharaoh, God instructs Moses to assemble the Israelites to bind them in an infinite bond with their deliverer. In the text Moses emphasizes: "I am making this covenant, with its oath, not only with you who are standing here with us today in the presence of the Lord our God but also with those who are not here today." That's us.

Interpreters of Jewish tradition throughout the centuries have taken "those not here today" to mean all the future generations. We all were included in this moment of promise. Our debt for having been liberated, that is to say for being alive, is to live a life of divine devotion through caretaking a lineage that is liberatory.

In our daily liturgy we proclaim: *L'dor vador nagid godlecha* ... "From generation to generation, we will tell of Your greatness..." The root of that greatness is liberation from oppression. The obligation of that liberation is ensuring all future generations are free.

Through the past few months, I have been trying to understand what today's moral failures mean for the next generation. What this generation's children will be saddled with and possible of.

As we watch with anguish and horror an entire generation of Palestinian children in Gaza suffer from famine and thirst, from the trauma of watching their loved ones be brutally killed, by being forced to endure amputations without anesthesia, as they are left orphaned and homeless, sleeping in the cold, wet mud we must ask ourselves: what is our responsibility to this generation? Are they too not the inheritors of G-d's promise of protection? Is G-d's greatness not also for them? Is the future not also theirs?

How do I understand my own children's future? My children sit in warmth and comfort, bellies full, with unimpeded access to any medical care they might need. They go to school and to the playground. I bring them to protests to call for ceasefire. We discuss at the dinner table my organizing Rabbis for Ceasefire. We surround them with Jewish life that includes solidarity with Palestinians, with all people. What does being part of a chain of transmission of Jewish traditions mean if not preparing them to be allies to their peers in Gaza as they grow? How do I even think about my own kids when children of Gaza are treated as they are? How do I prepare them to take up their ethical obligations?

From his prison cell before the Nazi's hanged him for his anti-fascist organizing, Pastor and anti-Nazi activist Dietrich Bonhoeffer wrote: "The ultimate question for a responsible person to ask is not how one is to extricate themselves heroically from the affair, but how the coming generation is to live."

Our actions in this moment will reverberate with a profound urgency for years to come. The covenant established between the divine and the human can be a path to healing and transformation and protection for the rising generation if we let it.

Despite what we might have wished, our failures are their burdens. Our children are saddled with the work of securing freedom and dignity for themselves and their comrades. They deserve the protection their ancestors merited. They deserve our dogged commitment to acting not just for today but for a million tomorrows

Lamentation:
How Can a Jew not Weep
for the Children of Gaza?
Jonathan Tilove

I never met my mother's father, Joseph Backer, who died in Philadelphia on June 6, 1943, eleven years to the day before I was born. What I did know was that he came from Bialystok, a city in northeast Poland that was then part of Russia; that he was a Bundist (a secular, Jewish democratic socialist) whose politics, like that of my other grandparents, defined his faith and my family's; that he had changed his name from Ezerkowsky to Backer (he was a baker) sometime before coming to America in 1908, and that he prized dissent. My Aunt Ruth would tell me with some amusement how on Yom Kippur, "Pop" would settle into window seat at the Schrafft's in Philadelphia and eat, for his fellow Jews to see, an act of quirky defiance that struck me, even as a child, as very, endearingly Jewish.

And that was about it until last year when I decided to visit my daughter, Aria, in Berlin and for us, together, to go to Bialystok. Aria was finishing her master's at Humboldt University. I had worked 45 years as a reporter with a special interest in race, and I was working on a memoir for Third World Press about how much that owed to the milieu I grew up in. My parents had a lifelong circle of friends, first generation American-born Jews, who came of age together in the Depression as Yipsels — members of the Young People's Socialist League — and stuck together the rest of their lives, becoming influential figures in the creation of a 20th Century American liberalism that enshrined what I thought of as Jewish values — a commitment to civil rights and civil liberties, an outrage with injustice and oppression, a welcoming of the stranger.

Berlin would give me a chance to see how Germany had confronted its Nazi past, and to go with Aria to Bialystok to see what more I could learn about where my grandfather and her great-grandfather had come from.

In preparing for my trip, I learned my grandfather was born Jossel Jeziorkowski in Wysokie Mazowieckie, a small town about an hour outside Bialystok, and that he was one of seven siblings (I didn't know he had any). I connected with newly discovered family in California, who twenty years ago had compiled a 15-page family history describing my grandfather as "a baker and a revolutionary (who) was exiled to Siberia by Czarist Russia, escaped and came to the US."

What I couldn't prepare for was that I would be departing for Berlin from Dulles Airport on the evening of Saturday, October 7, as news was breaking of the horrific Hamas attack on Israel, a spree of mayhem, bloodletting and hostage-taking.

Israel declared war on Hamas and by Monday, it was plain that it intended to make Gaza uninhabitable. "I have ordered a complete siege on the Gaza Strip," declared Yoav Gallant, the Israeli minister of defense. "There will be no electricity, no food, no fuel, everything is closed. We are fighting human animals and we are acting accordingly." The worst day for Jews since the Holocaust would lead to the worst days for the Palestinians since the Nakba. A catastrophe upon catastrophe, I told Aria.

I was born on June 6, 1954, the tenth anniversary of D-Day and in the shadow of the Holocaust, which bound Jews together amid a chastened world. In retrospect, my lifetime may have been the most halcyon period in Jewish, or at least, Jewish-American history. But now, it all seemed to be coming undone.

I'll admit, even in the best of times, I am my mother's son, a worrier, evidenced by the bags under my eyes in childhood snapshots. My 13th birthday (no bar mitzvah, then or since) fell two days into the Six Day War. Israel had just turned 19 and still seemed like David arrayed against the Goliath of the Arab World. As the Wilson Center summed it up, "in those six days, Israel defeated three Arab armies, gained territory four times its original size and became the preeminent military power in the region." It was an elixir for most American Jews, an answer, of sorts, to the Holocaust. When we talked about it in my seventh-grade social studies class, I felt the eyes of some of my classmates upon me, gleaming with a new respect. Did this mean I would no longer be picked last in gym class? I was, frankly, fine with the status quo. And I wasn't at all sure about the implications of Israel humiliating its enemies and occupying their territory. What happens, I wondered, when the bullied becomes the bully?

Berlin was tense on my arrival. There was security protecting Jewish sites and restricting Palestinian protests. Germany's laudable efforts to assume responsibility for the Holocaust had become a single-minded identification of Israel as the answer, and any criticism of Israel, even from Jews, let alone Palestinians, as intolerable anti-Semitism.

Poland

Poland had the largest Jewish population in Europe before theHolocaust. It is where the Holocaust claimed half its victims. And Bialyst ok was once one of the most Jewish places on Earth. In 1912, there were nearly 75,000 Jews living there, 75 percent of the population, and nearly as many Jews as lived in Palestine ten years later. I learned this from reading the book, Jewish Bialystok, by Tomasz Wisniewski, a writer, historian and filmmaker who, while not Jewish, has devoted himself to recognizing the Jewish history of the city where he lives and which is now home to only one a Jew, or two, depending on who you count.

Our first full day in Poland, we visited the remnants of the Jewish Cemetery in Wysokie Mazowieckie, a 49-minute train ride from Bialystok. Once home to 2,500 Jews, half the population, it is now without Jews. After visiting the remnants of the Jewish cemetery, Aria and I were caught in a downpour. In our rush to board a train back to Bialystok, we boarded going the wrong way. We got off at the first stop, the small town of Czyzew. We had an hour before the train returning to Bialystok would be there. There was a small convenience store by the station. We went in looking for hot coffee. No luck, and with a notably lukewarm reception, we waited for our train in the rain. It turned out the Jews from Wysokie Mazowieckie were taken in horse-drawn carts to Czyzew for transfer to the trains that would take them to Auschwitz or, nearer by, Treblinka.

Two days later, Aria and I disembarked the Bialystok-Warsaw train at Malkinia, one stop past Czyzew, looking for a taxi to take us the rest of the way. The only cab in evidence appeared to be empty. Aria, the more intrepid traveler, peered inside, saw the driver napping in the back seat, and roused him.

"Treblinka?" she asked.

"Treblinka," he replied. He spoke no English and we spoke no Polish, but we seemed to be communicating.

As we got going, Aria gave me a nudge. There was what appeared to me to be an apparition hovering alongside our driver. It was Adolf Hitler, in uniform, his left hand clutching his leather belt by its buckle, his right arm thrust forward in the Sieg Heil salute. My eyes widened. Aria redirected my gaze. There, on the dashboard, rested a book, face up, its cover image reflecting off the windshield. *Jak Hitler mógl wygrac wojne,* read the title. It was the Polish edition of a 2000 book by the American military historian Bevin Alexander, How Hitler Could Have Won the War. From Amazon: "Alexander's harrowing study shows how only minor tactical changes in Hitler's military approach could have changed the world we live in today." Harrowing. Indeed. Arriving at Treblinka, and realizing there was no obvious other way to get back to Malkinia, Aria asked our driver to return for us in three hours.

I'm not sure what I was expecting. What I was not expecting is that we would be the only ones there. It was an exceptionally beautiful fall day, with a bright sun and a gentle breeze. There is never an admission fee, and, since this was Monday, not even the 7 Polish zlotys fee for parking and toilets.

As we wondered where everybody was, we were startled to see a familiar face. It was Wisniewski, who I had come to call Tomek after Aria and I spent two hours with him the previous day in his small, crammed museum of Jewish Bialystok known as Miejsce — The Place. Tomek was accompanied by a Jewish man from Australia, his daughter, and infant grandson, who were all going to visit the grave of the man's great-grandmother, who died in 1921 at a Jewish cemetery outside Bialystok. The man offered me his black kippah for my visit.

And then they left and Aria and I truly had Treblinka all to ourselves, along with the 900,000 souls who perished there between July 1942 and the end of August 1943, a death toll second only to Auschwitz.

The Nazis had done their best to disguise Treblinka when it was killing Jews, and when it was done. Across five acres, there are 17,000 scattered stones — the number of Jews it could "exterminate" in a day. There are 216 gravestones bearing the names of the places they came from. The Bialystok marker was easy to find, and slightly bowed.

Uprisings at Treblinka in early August 1943 and in the Bialystok Ghetto two weeks later could not alter its fate, providing the very last Jews gassed and cremated at Treblinka. Those trains, arriving on August 18 and 19, carried 8,000 Jews.

When we visited Tomek at his museum, he had shown us *Castaways*, a beautiful short documentary he made in 2013 that told a story, recalled by eyewitnesses now grown old, about those last trains from Bailystok. As they passed through the small town of Lapy on the way to Treblinka, several dozen children were cast out, through small windows, in hopes someone might rescue them. According to the witnesses, only one was known to have survived, rescued and raised by a Polish Catholic family. She still lives in Lapy to this day, and had children of her own, but prefers to remain anonymous.

Within three months of my grandfather's death, the Jewish world he had known had been erased.

On our taxi ride back to the Malkinia station, *Jak Hitler* was no longer perched on the windshield. It now rested on the console between the two front seats. The next day we were on the train heading to Warsaw to visit the POLIN Museum of the History of Poland's Jews located on the site of what was once the Warsaw Ghetto. Ruminating on the trip, I was vexed by the argument that criticism of Zionism was necessarily anti-Semitism. I would have hoped that contemplation of the Holocaust might have prompted more troubled reflection about Israel's resort to collective punishment, children included, and the shunting hither and yon of Palestinian families.

We were sitting in the last row of our train car in our ticketed seats. A man arrived, about my age, and ordered the woman sitting in front of us to surrender the window seat. He had a tracheotomy, his hoarse voice laced with menace. We resumed our sotto voce conversation about the worsening situation in Gaza, and, while I did not notice it, Aria would later tell me, he was turning around in his seat to glare at me. After about 15 minutes he rose from his seat, approached me, and, one hand clutching his throat, berated me with a fusillade of Polish. I had no idea what he was saying but nodded along. He gestured for me to move, either to the empty seats across the aisle, or perhaps off the train altogether. And when I didn't budge, he reared back his right arm and then swung it forward, striking my chest with the back of his fist. No one on the train reacted, with the obvious exception of Aria, who issued an outraged and protective, "Hey!" Without budging, I stared at him and he stared at me. And, after an odd long moment, he walked off and exited the train car, getting off as it pulled into the next stop. It was Malkinia. The Treblinka stop.

The front page of the next morning's *New York Times* reported the deadliest air attacks on Gaza since the war began, bringing the death toll in the 19 days since October 7 to nearly 6,000 (according, as the Times noted, to the Hamas-run Ministry of Health) including 1,200 children. Alongside it was a story about how the impending Israeli ground invasion "could produce some of the fiercest street-to-street fighting since World War II."

Two hours into visiting the POLIN museum that afternoon, I was stopped still by a young woman staring at me from a sepia-toned 1930s photograph. She was the spitting image of Aria as a teenager. She was one of four girls in the photo who are identified as members of Hashomer Hatzair, a labor Zionist youth movement from Ejszyszki, a small town in what is now Lithuania. Aria's look-alike appears so alive, bright and present. She doesn't look like an image from a dead past. It was only six months later, as I was completing this essay, that I could bear to find out the terribly predictable fate of Ejszyszki. On September 27, 1941, 3,446 Jews — 989 men, 1,636 women, and 821 children — were taken to the Jewish cemetery and executed by the Einsatzkommando 3a, a notably zealous Nazi mobile killing squad.

Ninety minutes after my encounter with Aria's double, my long day at the POLIN drawing to a close, there amid images of the Holocaust, I came face to face with myself —my precise likeness in a boy of about nine at Auschwitz. He was wearing a yellow cloth Star of David pinned to his jacket and the cross expression that was all my own at that age. It's me. And next to me, who I presume to be a little brother, is an exact replica of my sister's son, my nephew, Steven, at that age. An older woman behind them is clutching her heart. The frame is filled with people, standing amid trees, all still fully dressed in hats and coats. They must have just arrived. Below the image is a quote from Auschwitz commandant Rudolf Hoss: "The most important thing, of course, was to maintain as much peace and quiet as possible during the process of arriving and undressing."

The Israeli war on Gaza had hit its awful stride, killing Palestinian children at the rate of more than 60 a day. In the name of security, it was making every Jew on the planet less safe, none more so than those living in Israel, and all of us implicitly complicit. Trauma begetting trauma, in perpetuity, I wept for my doppelganger and his little brother. I wept for the children of Gaza being slaughtered in his, and our, name. I wept as a Jew. I wept for the Jews.

Addendum: The brothers in the photo were not identified by name. But nearly a month after I finished this piece, I learned, in a most improbable way, who they are. I was watching a *60 Minutes* report on May 19 on the opening of a new show in New York, *Here There Are Blueberries*, based on an album of photos, taken by an SS man, of the Nazi officers and their secretaries relaxing in their off hours at Auschwitz. The *60 Minutes* report, and the play, also included a photo from another album of Auschwitz photos also taken by an SS man. It depicted Jews, just arrived from Hungary by cattle car in the waning days of the war, waiting briefly in a grove of trees, not certain what fate would befall them, before being marched to the gas chambers. It is the precise photo I fixated on in Warsaw. The boys are Reuven and Gershon Fogel. Seated on the ground behind them is their mother, Leah. They were identified in the photo by the boys' older sister, Irene Fogel Weiss, now 93, who is interviewed on *60 Minutes*. Weiss and her older sister, Serena, were put to work and survived. Her mother and her father, Meyer; older brother, Moshe, and younger sister, Edith, along with Reuven and Gershon, all perished at Auschwitz.

On Parenthood and Genocide:
A New Mother and Scholar of Forced Displacement Writes about Israel's Mass Murder of Palestinian Children in Gaza

Heba Gowayed

As the sun streams through the windows of our New York apartment, I watch our now five-month-old son grab his newly found feet. He sways as he chats with the baby looking back at him in the mirror attached to the play gym. He breaks into a wide-mouthed smile when he turns and catches my gaze. My chest constricts with the enormity of my gratitude for his existence and joy.

And, as I have often done in the last 100 days, I think of Gaza.

I think of the mother who, like me, struggled to have a child only to then lose him to the flippant brutality of bombs dropped from the sky. Of the father desperately clutching his soot-covered daughter, her fat arms and feet dangling limp against his chest. Of another father who tried to wrap a cookie into his son's lifeless hand. He had been so excited to find his son a treat at the market only to come home to find him dead. Of the babies lined up in the NICU of a Gaza hospital under attack, who would soon likely not be wrapped in the muslin of a swaddle as my baby was, but in a white *kafan* (a burial shroud).

For the past 100 days we have witnessed a massacre of children, of childhoods. Of the roughly 24,000 Palestinians who have been killed, almost 10,000 are children. Each had a name. A favorite color. A favorite toy. Each cackled at a parent's funny face.

The horrors befalling children of Gaza do not stop with death. Another 8,663 Gazan children have been injured. Each day, 10 children lose one or both of their legs — their limbs often amputated without anesthetic. Israeli forces have stripped young boys naked and paraded them in public. An estimated 25,000 children have lost a mother, a father — or both.

I am haunted by the images and videos of parents in Gaza with their children, by the love and grief comprising these figures. I am haunted because for the past decade I have worked with people who continue to endure the toll of war and displacement long after the end of violence. I am haunted because I am also the daughter of people who as children sheltered from Israeli bombs.

But most of all, and along with other parents who protest against the genocide and the mass murder of children in their identity as parents, I am haunted because I am a mother. Because I know what it is to feel a baby grow against my body, kick and hiccup against my ribs. Because I know the anxiety of watching a newborn's chest rise and fall, the vastness of the dreams I hold for my son, the lengths I'd go for his joy, that there is nothing I wouldn't do to protect him. I am haunted because if for some reason my son did not rise from his nap, I do not know what would become of me.

As a world we have failed the children of Gaza. We have failed our fellow parents. It is not a new failure. The vast majority of the 1.1 million children in Gaza were born behind a 17-year-old blockade which even in utero saw them as a danger to their colonizer, their lives and freedoms expendable for the sake of its stability. It's something we've seen time and again with the Israeli military. After the 2014 assault on Gaza, the Obliterated Families project reported that one-fourth of the 2,200 Palestinians killed were children, with 1,000 other children permanently disabled.

We have long acquiesced to Palestinian children living in these conditions, to our tax dollars being sent to build the technology of their confinement. I live in a country whose leaders have long deemed Arab children like my son as less than human. In Yemen, in Syria and Iraq, in Libya, in Palestine — Arab children, our children, are simply ok to kill.

Against the horror of this assault, Gazan parental love, the most natural thing in the world, is resistance. On November 3, Doaa, a Gazan mother of two, and an Arabic teacher, tweeted a photo of her five-year-old daughter beaming, holding a cupcake and wearing a sparkly tiara. She was proud to have managed a makeshift celebration for her daughter's birthday in the midst of the violence, writing "her happiness was worth the world." When Doaa was killed along with her other daughter 24 hours later, the image went viral.

Someone compiled videos of Gazan men playing with babies covered in soot to say, "Look at how gentle our men are; look at how they are not terrorists." As the daughter of a doting Arab father, I watched these videos and felt caught between my recognition of their sweet nothings and my offense at the need to share them.

I am angry any person would have to distract a baby covered in soot. That any of these images of parental love and resistance exist is testament to Gazan strength and endurance. The photographs and videos are produced because grieving parents allow journalists to train their cameras on them as they kiss their baby's eyes, kiss their baby's feet goodbye. I am struck by the desperate rage of it, the unwillingness to break. I am reminded of Black mothers in the American south like Mamie Till insisting on open casket funerals to show their children's mutilated bodies at the hand of white supremacists, their decades-long oppressors. The hope is that the world has a shred of shame, that if they look maybe they would be moved to act, to stop the violence. "Do not look away," the videos and photographs instruct us. The parents are cognizant that what they have endured is too much for the rest of us to passively consider. I must admit, this piece about their loss is the hardest thing I have penned in a long career of writing. I know I can never do justice to the depths of this parental love and loss.

The crime of genocide is the crime of destroying a nation, a people. In Gaza, multiple generations of families have been killed at once, giving rise to a new acronym, WCNSF: Wounded Child No Surviving Family. I have never had a fear of dying before I had my son. If something were to happen to me, I'd count on my loved ones to take care of him. They'd know the airplane sounds he likes, how he likes to be burped. I'd count on them to remember me to him. But what if they were all gone, too? The massacre in Gaza is so much more than an aggregate count of lives. It is the loss of collective memories held in those lives — of events, of people, of places. A loss for which generations and generations to come will continue to pay the price.

In the face of a colonizer intent on the destruction of their nation, of 75 years of unrelenting violence, Palestinians have insisted on *sumud*, unwavering perseverance. That they will be free in their land. That they will grow and bear fruit like the olive trees that they plant.

Gazan children deserve more than survival. They deserve more than to simply be unmolested by the whims of tyrants. They deserve futures, joyful futures. They deserve to babble and giggle with their parents. They deserve to live free, from the river to sea.

II

The Secrets of the Victors

(the only fair fight is the one that is won
—Anglo-Saxton Proverb)

Haki R. Madhubuti

forever define the enemy as less than garbage,
his women as whores & gutter scum,
their children as thieves & beggars,
the men as rapists, child molesters & cannibals,
their civilization as savage and
beautifully primitive.

as you confiscate the pagan's land, riches & women
curse them to your god for not being productive,
for not inventing barbed wire and DDT,
perpetually portray the *natives*
as innocent & simple-minded while eagerly
preparing to convert them to *your way.*

dispatch your merchants with
tins & sweets, rot gut & cheap wines.
dispatch your priests armed with
words of fear, conditional love and
fairy tales about strangers dying for you.
dispatch your military
to protect your new labor pool.
if there is resistance
or any show of defiance
act swiftly & ugly & memorable.
when you kill a man
leave debilitating fear in the hearts of his
father, brothers, uncles, friends & unborn sons.
if doubt exists as to your determination
wipe the earth with his
women, girl children & all that's sacred;
drunken them in bodacious horror.

upon quiet, summon the ministers to
bless the guilty as you publicly
break their necks.

after their memories fade intensify the teaching.
Instruct your holy men
to curse violence   while
proclaiming the Land Safe
introducing
the thousand-year Reign of the Victors
as your Scholars
re-write the history.

Note: My interest in Israel/Occupied Palestine goes back to 1962 upon meeting Professor Eugene Feldman at the DuSable Museum in Chicago, who educated me about Occupied Palestine. My visit to Israel/Occupied Palestine took place in the 1980s as the guest of the Original African Hebrew Israelites of Dimona. They took me to Gaza and the West Bank. I purchased the books of the great poet Mahmoud Darwish and wrote a poem for him, "A Poem for a Poet," that was published in one of my books. I also wrote a poem about the Beirut Massacre (September, 1982) in Sabra and Shatila.

Gaza Suite

Tony Medina

No cause, no God, no abstract idea can
justify the mass slaughter of innocents.
                              —Edward Said

Palestine

What will future archeologists make
    Of this in the land promised to fig trees,
Sand & the scorching sun? Where Jesus the
    Nazarene was born—where olive trees

    Ancient as the oldest of grandfathers
Wrenched from their roots by the forked tongues of cranes
    Coarse as confiscated land where mothers
Have wept & wailed for husbands, brothers &
    Babies in houses with no windows, forlorn.

What would those diggers make of a girl's skull cracked
    In mid-scream by bone & brick & bits of
Missile shells? Would a young apprentice look
    Up, squinting, & say—*that was a school, once.*

Seven Steps to Heaven Haiku

If every bomb
Appeared in the sky a dove
Shrapnel into rain

If vengeance vanquished
From the cursed lips of weak men
An idea never taking root

If every tank vanished
If by chance a miracle
Peace reclaims the land

If laughter broke out
Like wars fought with satire's

Pugilist punning

What room would there be
For anger what bitter root
Not allowed to stretch

Its tentacles
Through the hearts of men hardened
By indifference

What will we bequeath
Our children if not a world
Evermore human

Gaza Stripped

Somewhere in this land
Of broken teeth
And razor wire smile
A skinny boy hurls
A rock at a tank.

In response to that
Offhand knock, the tank
Aims and shoots,
Obliterating every inch
Within a mile of that smile.

In another part of
What once used to be
That town, children scream
So loud you can't hear them.
The shelling is so rapid,
Persistent and steady,
Each bomb blast
A lung's intake of air—
So black and heavy
It might as well be a boot.

Palestine

Let my blood tell you the story
Of what they did to my land

The bones the sea spit up
From the sloping sands
How they planted stones in
Our mouths so that nothing
Will grow, barren as blood-soaked palms
Along spent shell no-go farms.

Each night the wind carries
Our voices—faraway screams—the
Crying & whining & whimpering
Teapot simmer kids contribute, until

A bomb punctuates the air,
Erasing all confusion. Death
Comes, like a census taker, with its
Muddy, burlap satchel, collecting

Each wail, frozen, in
The phosphorous trickle, dully
Wafting from leaf to leaf, like
The pale pallor of a listless child.

Tanka

Let us always re-
Member: It is not just the
Body that never
Forgets—nor the olive trees—
But the land also keeps score.

Gaza Stripped

Paradise comes in bits and pieces, strips peeled
From the flesh of olive trees, coarse as sand in veins.
Scentless gas bombs like ghost hands weld eyes and mouths sealed.
The sky is a vast coffin lid of bloodstains.

Trees older than death ripped out like clumps of hair.
Gray buildings bulldozed while children sleep and pray,
Scatter like pigeons into a lion's lair,
Trapped in a place where not even God could stay.

What rises from the earth, pockmarked through concrete,
Cannot be chewed up and spit out by tank teeth;
Will not be mashed down by the steel heel of defeat.
Faith, once crucified, emerges from the heath.

Hope found in stones thrown at the blank stares of walls.
Black smoke of anguish clouds the land where peace falls.

Tanka

Imagine a world
Where bouquets overwhelm bombs
Sunshining the day
Voices gather like flowers
Blooming with something to say

Touch

Preeta lives next door
She is Palestinian
Our houses don't touch
I push my wrist through the fence
My open hand holds a doll

—*Naamah*—Israel (girl)

Ramallah Rumble

Jaddi's olive tree
Is taller than our house
And older than me
Trembles at the sound of tanks
Holding tightly to its leaves

—*Vajid*—Palestine (boy)

Azzah Azzah

I'd like to live in a world
Where the sun doesn't have
To have a reservation

Where water is not
Out on parole
And food is not exiled

Or exhumed from the dry
Mouths of babies
Whose bellies peel

Like hard mud in the open
Air rented away
To tourists

Arafat Airstrip, Gone

I will say goodbye
    To the planes
        By waving my hand
        In the air

I will say goodbye
    To my hand
        By watching it
        Fall off my wrist

Cartography of Grief

I wish I could draw a map
Of the headlines rattling inside
My brain like soundbites
Or the cracked chyron silence
Israel Invades Gaza
War Pushes Tensions to Breaking Point
War Spawns Waves of Refugees
I wish I could draw a map
Of the images terrorizing my tube
Tanks cutting across sand
Orange yellow flames flaring

Bullets puncture the pockmarked
Rubble of hospitals schools & mosques
As bricks pour from the black
Face of sky

I wish I could draw a map
From my head to my heart
How anguish stuns the tears
That want to come

I wish I could draw a map
Of the children of Palestine
How they wait for the silence
That never comes

How they crawl like ants
Out of the rubble of their broken city
Lost in a sea of smoke & flames
Climb over the crumbled bricks & bones
The burned bodies of home

How they manage through
Manmade craters and girders
Split & spiraling & sprung
Through the cracked face of concrete

To find a clear flat space
In the wreckage, kneel
Eastward, pressing their
Foreheads to the singed tar
Of their tiny bit of earth

& pray

Casualty Report

More than 10,000 children killed
By Israeli airstrikes

28, 064 Palestinians killed
In Gaza

386 school buildings
Damaged—25 gone

Israeli blockade of the
Gaza Strip restricts
Live-saving aid—

No food, medical supplies,
Sanitation or water

Many die of hunger
Many die of neglect
Many die of silence

Many die of indifference
Many die as the world
Ignores the children's cries

Rafah

Will a roadside bomb make confetti of my flesh
Will a hand grenade scramble my brains
Will Molotov cocktail flames cling to each pore
Will my skin evaporate in the wind
Will there be a yard sale for my limbs
Will a little girl's splattered blood cleanse me of sin

Rafah

I would like my blood to stay where it is
I'm used to the smooth of my skin

I would hate for it to be
Burned off my bones by the blast

Of a bomb or the split brick of my house
Collapsed like a heart clogged with fury

Triptych: Angles of Anguish

I

Modern soldiers shoot
As if playing video
Games, then record shots
On cellphones, big-game bragging—
Showoff the dead like trophies

II

Twelve thousand children
Plowed into earth bombarded
Twelve thousand flowers
Seeded by indifference
Pollinating resistance

III

What they don't tell you
What's not recorded for news
Is the screaming drowned
Out by bombs that rattle bones
Burst eardrums steal parents' breath

Because the Sky

Because the sky hasn't always been black
Smoke peppered with dumb bombs
Because the sun hasn't always wept
At the sudden silence of sunbirds

Because my little bit of confiscated earth
Hasn't always swallowed my children
Snatched from the womb
Because this battered body that once pumped

Blood virile as a raging river stream
Hasn't always been sacrificed at the altar
Of vengeance, indifference & greed
Because this heavy heart that once rode

The horseback of hope galloping
Galaxies of dreams
Because I refuse to let them turn my spirit
To stone, generations of desire into a tomb

Because resistance is all I ever had
In this hour of chaos riddled with bullets
Because I insist on planting poems
Even as tank teeth gnaw and jaw and law

Because what will spring from cement rubble
Splattered with my blood—my grandfather's
Olive tree—stately and dignified—yet with Ata
All due humility in the face of God
Its leaves like flags waving in the wind
On branches that do not break
But bend & bow
Centuries from now

BG

Mursalata Muhammad

Seven.
She holds
tightly to slivers
of memory. Each one,
a fraying fabric - losing its
color and sensory connection to the
deep rootedness of what made her a

child.
Each thread
unraveling the childhood
collection of small priceless
gifts mother cobbled together. A
smile. A wink. A song mother
only sang in the BG (before genocide)
time.

Circle of Fifths for Gaza

Gabriel I. Green

from all this death my soul hurt
my soul hurt from all this loss
all this loss my soul hurt tired
soul hurt tired all this loss burns
this loss burns soul hurt tired raged
hurt tired raged this loss burns hot
loss burns hot hurt tired raged death
tired raged death loss burns hot from
burns hot from tired raged death my
raged death my burns hot from all
hot from all raged death my soul
death my soul hot from all this
from all this death my soul hurt

Look How They Blame the Hungry for Swallowing Their Anger (after Tariq Luthun)

Gabriel I. Green

And I suppose hunger by a different name might be called desperation. Desperation by a different name might be called radical. Radical by a different name might be called extremist. Extremist by a different name might be called a terrorist. A terrorist by a different name might be called revolutionary. Revolutionary by a different name might be called incivility. Incivility by a different name might be called an occupation. An occupation by a different name might be called protection. Protection by a different name might be called colonization. Colonization by a different name might be called a chokehold. A chokehold by a different name might be called a slow death. A slow death by a different name might be called a mercy.

And what is merciful about a slow death? What is civil about this protective chokehold of an occupation that makes radicals out of the desperate? Or alchemizes terrorists from the hungry?

Her People Named Her

Ezra Hyland

Her People named her Afaaf (chaste, virtuous, decent, pure)
The elders even the children called her Ata (a gift from god)
Her smile sweet as white raisins

Then the soldiers came
They named her whore
A night between her thighs paradise

Her people gone
She cries
Presses the small red button
Praying her way to heaven
Will be paved with the bodies of those
Who condemned her to hell

Such strange symmetry
We are the same
No way to tell bomber from bombed
by the bits of flesh and blood and bone
Mere confetti in death's parade

Ayat Akhras, 16

Aneb Kgositsile

This life that is left to us
is that of spirits suspended in the air,
moving like ghosts among the stone skeletons and
rubble of our demolished homes.

Rising in joy to morning chores or troubles
is the life of human beings –
those who truly inhabit the earth,
who mark some patch of ground
with their trials and triumphs.

No spot of land sighs our names.
No crevice, even,
says, "Ayat Akhras, I belong to you."

This life of no life
has prepared me for death.
I cover myself in our people's shawl—
symbol of loss and longing –
and begin the ritual.
I will give my life for the lives I take.
I pray. I ask my fiancé's forgiveness.
I will not be his bride in summer.
I strap the sacrificial fire to my breast.
In calm, I walk into the work-day rush
of their city.
I meet the eyes of those about to die with me.
I breathe my last.
Wafu Idris, sister,
I am coming.

Wafu Idris and Ayat Akhras were the first and second women suicide martyrs in the Palestinian struggle to end Israeli occupation and win Palestinian statehood.

Possession Dance
Visiting the Occupied Territories
Aneb Kgositsile

Can't sit down.
No, I can't sit down.
Can't sit still
because I cannot contain
knowledge of such outrages --
because the chest is not
hollow enough,
because the viscera swells
and chokes my breath.
Must escape this trance, fly
out of this prison of lies,
swing, kick, whirl, thrash,
flail against this Israeli war, against
the horrors of torture, the
pain of wounded children;
flail and thrash until the
truth speaks to your heart.
Must dance, arch, heave out
the knowing of all these disasters.
Can't sit still, no, I can't sit down.
Can't sit down, no, I can't sit down....

*This poem was inspired by a visit to a hospital in Gaza, where we talked with
children who had been wounded with Israeli soldiers' rubber bullets. The image
of a possession dance is associated with the same trip to Palestine/Israel. At the
Wailing Wall, there was an elderly woman who was dovening. I watched as
slowly her swaying back and forth in prayer turned into a dance.*

Genocide in the Name of Peace
Michael Simanga

1.
today
concrete
ash
floats
again
like
falling
snow
from
heavenly
skies
fast
loud
machines
laughing
at
starving
children

2.
centuries
stories
myth
tales
lies
heroic
conquests
gods
murder
destroying
cultures
take
land
take
dreams
snatch
lives
thank
gods

3.
dusty
roads
empty
fields
memories
children
running
kicking
soccer
balls
laughing

4.
god
wants
what
from
us
buried
under
history
houses
hospitals
schools
markets
mosques
churches
temples

5.
powerful
countries
do
god
work
send
bombs
gifts
cash
to
friends
no

food
water
shelter
medicine
freedom
to
people
doing
gods
work

6.
god
is
not
silent
and
the
wounded
displaced
hungry
grieving
know
god
cannot
be
we
will
not
be

Talking to Hamas
Alice Walker

Huda Naim, democratically
elected official,
I do not know how it goes with you
and your children
but every day I am thinking of you.
Did you know that before we left the US
our government spokespeople
told us: you mustn't speak to anyone
from Hamas
as if we were little children
who must be warned
not to speak to strangers.
However,
the moment we heard:
to talk to us
every single woman
rushed to see who it was.
I had to laugh, we were so typical
In that way. One of the reasons I have enjoyed
so much
being what I am. Curious. A woman. Forgetful of advice.
And imagine our surprise
our delight,
when the dreaded "terrorist" we were warned
against—that we envisioned in battle fatigues
and shouldering a long black
rocket launcher—
turned out to be you:
portly, smiling, your eyes looking
directly into ours.
And what did we talk about: mostly
our children. Your five. Our twos and threes.
Or one. How we wanted, all of us, a sane world
for them.
Ah, Huda Naim, how I hope one day
that you will meet
our Israeli sister, Nurit, and our brother,
Miko. I know you will like them, as I do.
And the young ones refusing to join

the occupation army
but going instead
to jail
and the old ones, like Uri, somehow
holding on.
There are so many good people
In your tortured land.
And I wonder if you know
Natalya,
the poet who was with us
later
in Ramallah.
Our Natalya who writes poems to the world and emails to me
as the bombs fall around her sheltering
place: "Alice, I cannot breathe. Our hearts
have stopped."
I sit, and wring my hands,
at last old enough and sad enough,
and pathetic enough in my impotence
to do this.
Huda Naim, I pray you and your children
your whole family
all your worlds
are safe.
Yet how can it be
with Israeli bombs
and now assault rifles
and tanks
demolishing
your neighborhoods?
I would weep
but tears seemed dried out
by the terror and love
I feel for you.

The world has awakened at last
to your true face, Huda Naim.
The world has woken
up. Though it is so used
to being asleep.
The world is standing, shouting its rude awakening
in the street.
That is the profit
I see, so far,

from the globally witnessed
fire sale
of your people's pain.

Still, I have seen the world wake up
before. When it has woken up before
it has moved.

The Slain Children of Palestine Hold Council in Paradise

Alice Walker

Who knew death would be like this?
A young boy considers reconnecting a limb
and looks down thoughtfully
at an eye. An eye that looks
casually around Palestine
which turns out to be
everywhere.
Who knew
we would learn so much
and that the journey—
from the way things look—
will never end?
They are still fighting
and killing us
below. They do not know
we never die.
But do *they*?
And is this the way
life punishes them?
Never to be known for what
they give to the world
which is a lot:
but by what they take?
What message
to our parents
our schoolmates
our friends?
How much love they have
for us, the fallen,
how much suffering
our deaths
have caused!
If only we could drop
that feather
promised to Yoko Ono
by John Lennon!*
Announcing the promised

Realm of Being
that does not ever disappoint
or disappear!
We are the lucky ones
gone on to Glory.
How do we judge
those who murdered us?
How do we say to our families
this is not the end?
That it is Life's deathless
breath that now is
holding us,
in a peace
that has no name
or form;
inexhaustible Life
that opens once again
in dying:
Life that witnesses
everything
forever:
and is widely flexible
in its Eternity.

It is said that John Lennon promised his beloved Yoko that if he found whatever "heaven" is, after his death, he would let her know by dropping a feather.

Hope
Alice Walker

Hope never
to covet
the neighbors' house
with the fragrant
garden
   from which a family
has been
        driven by your soldiers;
mother, father,
grandparents,
the toddler and
the dog
now homeless:
huddled, holding on
to each other,
stunned
and friendless
beneath you
in the street:
sitting on
cobblestones
as if on the sofas
inside
that you have decided
to clean, recover and
keep.
Hope never
to say yes
to their misery.
Hope never to gaze
down into their faces
from what used to be
their rooftop.
Hope never to believe
this robbery
will make you a better
citizen of your new
country
as you unfurl and wave

its recent
flag
that has been given
to assure you
of this impossibility

You Ask for a Poem
Marilyn Kallet

You ask me for a poem about current events: babies and
Toddlers slaughtered at Kibbutz Be'eri, war in Gaza. I say

No, I have no poem, coward that I am. But my heart says
Sister, you know how to grieve. You know your heart still beats

And little ones do not. Aged ones have stopped
Short. I have not walked these killing fields but I embody

A voice that tries to soar, to descend into
The wreckage, voice that is only sound yearning

To show love and care, throat that can bemoan the loss
Of every life in Gaza, each drop of blood spilled.

I have entered gas chambers as a tourist, to see what
My relatives endured before the end at Terezín.

But this is now, Israel, all of us, and we grieve
Together and beg the wisest ones to take charge,

Stop the blood-letting and save little heads
From being chopped and big ones from pontificating

While more of us are lost.
Yisgadal v'yistkadash sh'mei raba…

Glory to those who bring peace where others
Cannot find a way. Condolences to every family

That has lost a loved one in this carnage.
Let us create, vow to love more, every way.

Grief is our teacher.
Let us dedicate our time to friendship

And peace.
May it be so.

III

Births of Two Nations:
Global Gaslighting and Reproductive Injustice for Palestinian, Black and Indigenous Families

J. Raya Bell

If you're not careful, the newspapers will have you hating the people being oppressed, and loving those doing the oppressing.
- Malcolm X

We remind ourselves that the pen is mightier than the sword and it appears, even as we write this, like so much hubris. Writing does not shield any of us in the face of the weapons and equipment of war. We are certain this meagre offering will not shield any Black, Indigenous, or Palestinian children from the annihilation visited on them from state, military, police, and institutional violence. Yet, the pen is our weapon of choice; it is the pen that we have been given to wield; our writing is all we have. And until they practice war no more, we are off "to the riverside" to pick up this sword and shield and brandish them as best we can.

In any essay collection dedicated to children, it is wise to look at the conditions surrounding the birthing of children. Simultaneously, when we examine issues connected to race and ethnicity, it is wise to examine the circumstances surrounding childbirth. After all, the social construction of race is intimately connected to social decisions made around childbirth. The Virginia House of Burgesses 1662 act establishing that the child inherits the condition of the enslaved mother arguably is among the most infamous of such decisions. Thus, when we have a collection dedicated to children in a situation of intense racism and genocide—as we see in the case of Israeli treatment of Palestinians—we must look at childbirth as a place where injustice can be seen and resisted.

This essay about reproductive justice in Black, Indigenous and Palestinian communities is established on the fact that the two nations - Israel and the United States – are settler colonial states, and although academics and activists will be punished for saying this about Israel, we note that almost every Israeli, British, and American national leader has themselves named Israel as a settler colonial state. Hence, we address the idea that we are being gaslighted when pointing out these obvious conditions. This essay explains how reproductive justice is in a specific relationship to a settler colonial project, as well as the ways that reproductive injustice is demonstrated for Black, Indigenous, and Palestinian communities. The essay ends with the desire that efforts for solidarity around reproductive justice between Black, Indigenous, and Palestinian peoples can be viewed as aspirational for our children's resistance, resilience, hope, and liberation.

In 1915, D.W. Griffith released the horrifically racist propaganda film, *The Birth of a Nation*, trying to justify the US as a white supremacist nation and lifting up the Ku Klux Klan in the process. During the same year, Herbert Samuel, who would become the first High Commissioner for British Palestine 5 years later, wrote *The Future of Palestine*, arguing for establishment of a British colony that would eventually give birth to an independent Jewish state.2 These events from 1915 are not the only occasions tying the beginning of Israel as a modern state to the conditions of the birth and identity of the US. In fact, both nations have been borne from white supremacist settler colonialism and its attendant doctrines of discovery.

Regarding Israel, there are many complexities about the historical relationships between Palestinians, Israelis, and the land that both groups call home. Hence, there is an obvious worry of oversimplifying the situation. As Palestinian poet Mourid Barghouti famously noted:

It is easy to blur the truth with a simple linguistic trick: start your story from "Secondly." Yes, this is what Rabin did. He simply neglected to speak of what happened first. Start your story with "Secondly," and the world will be turned upside-down. Start your story with "Secondly," and the arrows of the Red Indians are the original criminals, and the guns of the white men are entirely the victims. It is enough to start with "Secondly," for the anger of the Black man against the white to be barbarous. Start with "Secondly," and Gandhi becomes responsible for the tragedies of the British.3

Because of this persistent worry about oversimplifying the Palestinian-Israeli conflict, there is also a worry that propagandists will purposefully complicate and obfuscate the situation to gaslight people into thinking that we cannot obtain *any* clear and settled knowledge of the matter(s). This is then used to say we cannot condemn certain actions, or states of affairs, or demand revolutionary change. History did not begin on 7 October with the attack by Hamas and the most recent escalation of conflict in Gaza. And certainly, for Black, Indigenous, and Palestinian communities the circumstances of colonialism in general, and reproductive injustice in particular, are extensive, historical, and relentless. This essay is an attempt to frame these different histories in terms of their comparable connections to the project and structures of settler colonialism.

All writing about Palestine seems to begin, *de rigueur*, with a ludicrous and ignored stipulation that pro-Palestinian is not anti-Semitic, that anti-Zionism is neither anti-Semitic nor anti-Israel. Regarding these discriminations, Lila Abu-Lughod reminds us that "Anti-Semitism is about who one is; anti-Zionism is about a political project."4 And yet the reaction to even a hint of pro-Palestinian, anti-Zionist, anti-oppression, pro-liberation analysis is met with global gaslighting. While we witness and want to speak out against the realities of oppression and genocide, we are told it is something else; it is conveyed to us that what we behold is not what our eyes see.

One of the places this gaslighting happens is with respect to the fact of Israel as a settler colonial white supremacist state. Whatever other controversies or reasonable disagreements there may be when it comes to Palestinian-Israeli relations, it is straightforwardly true that the state of Israel is a creation of settler colonialism. In fact, the founders of the state of Israel were very open about this. In August 1897, at the First Zionist Congress in Basel, the Basel Program was unanimously adopted, with goal number one being, "The expedient promotion of the settlement of Jewish agriculturists, artisans, and businessmen in Palestine." Originally written in German, this is also translated as promoting "the *colonization* of Palestine by Jewish agricultural and industrial workers" (emphases added).5 In either case, we clearly have a statement of settler colonial intentions.

Also in 1897, Theodor Herzl wrote an article on "The Jewish Colonial Trust" which was formed in 1899. The first chairman of the Trust's Board of Directors was David Wolffsohn, Herzl's successor as the leader of the Zionist Movement. This was followed by the Second Aliyah – a mass immigration to the colony of Palestine - from which most of the founders of the state of Israel came. Including the subsequent Third Aliyah, these settlements were enacted under British support until Britain passed that role to Israel in 1948. It should, therefore, be unsurprising that while beginning under supervision of the settler colonial state of Great Britain, Israel's settler colonialism is incontrovertibly an extension of the Doctrine of Discovery.

The Doctrine of Discovery was a set of policies, practices, and protocols put in place from the 1450s onward which advocated for Indigenous genocide and African enslavement in the name of new colonies. The settlement of North and South America was established with European imperial powers enshrinement in settler colonial legal frameworks of various doctrines of dispossession: The Doctrine of Discovery (European Christians' unfettered right to Indigenous lands); *Terra Nullius* (Indigenous lands are legally unoccupied until the arrival of a colonial presence, and can therefore become the property of the colonizing power through effective occupation); and, *Dum Diversas* (perpetual enslavement by European Christians of Africans, Muslims, and any deemed pagans by the settlers).

In Palestine, just as in Euro-American white supremacist settler colonialism, there are terra nullius arguments, like those based in the works of Thomas Hobbes and John Locke in the founding of the USA. For instance, the first prime minister of Israel, David Ben-Gurion, said about the founding of the state of Israel:

> I believed then as I do today that we had a clear title to this country. Not the right to take it away from others (there were no others) but the right and the duty to fill its emptiness, restore life to its barrenness, to recreate a modern version of our own nation. And I felt we owed this effort not only to ourselves but to the land as well.

In an even more direct statement of Israel's colonial, genocidal intent, the fourth prime minister of Israel, Golda Meir, stated, "There was no such thing as Palestinians… they did not exist."7 When examining these histories, Arwa Mahdawi reminds us that we don't actually need a PhD in Middle Eastern studies to understand the situation in Jerusalem, the West Bank, and Gaza.8 Just like we don't need a doctorate in critical race theory to understand the situation of Black and Indigenous Americans' reproductive health injustices. What is required is close reading, critical thinking, careful analysis, and honest reflection. It helps if we also begin with a commitment to the norms and principles of human rights which undergird the reproductive justice framework.

Thinking about Palestinian relations to the state of Israel, or Black or Indigenous relations to the US, we are further reminded that this is the circumstance of peoples relating to a state that is founded and predicated on their demise. Furthermore, in both cases, the US and Israel are established on the demise of Black, Indigenous, or Palestinian individuals within their lifetimes and within their communities over generations. Given this, a focus on reproductive justice is necessary. In other words, just as understanding the *production* of the states of Israel and the US is necessary to recognizing their nature as white supremacist settler colonial states, so too is understanding the maintenance and *reproduction* of those settler colonial structures over time. Given our focus, it should be unsurprising that we believe that reproduction of settler colonialism requires reproductive injustice and, thus, that reproductive justice must be seen as a site of resistance against settler colonialism and white supremacy.

> I was born a Black woman / and now / I am become a
> Palestinian
> - June Jordan, *Moving Towards Home*, 1982

The reproductive justice framework was developed in the 1990s by African American and POC women to shift the narrative on maternal and child health away from a narrow pro-choice and abortion access focus to broader recognition of the associations between reproductive freedoms and antiracism efforts. The key principle put in place in the reproductive justice framework was acknowledgement of the ways racial, economic, and cultural systems of oppression for Black, Indigenous, and other non-white women were part of their reproductive health outcomes. The core values of the reproductive justice movement were inspired by and are embedded in a human rights framework:

- ✓ The right to have full autonomy over our bodies.
- ✓ The right to have or not have children.
- ✓ The right to birth and parent our children with dignity.
- ✓ The right to live and raise a family in a safe and healthy environment.

Reproductive injustice in Black and Indigenous American, and Palestinian communities is the degree to which these rights are not met as evidenced by the dismal statistics of maternal and child morbidity and mortality.

In reaction to the Hamas attacks on 7 October 2024, and the Israeli military response, a public letter was written and signed on 26 October titled, "Childhood Researchers and Students Call for Immediate Ceasefire in Gaza." It was reported that 33 children were killed in the initial attacks. At the point when the public letter was circulated, 3,000 children had died. Now, in late April, the number of children killed in the current Gaza conflict is closer to 14,000. The letter says, "Palestinian children have names, families, stories, and dreams, yet they are facing global and local brutalities that reduce them to anonymous numbers."9 Even without considering the equally appalling numbers of children maimed and injured at this time in the conflict, the deaths of children represent one of the horrors of reproductive injustice, as each child's family has been directly denied the right to live and raise that child in a safe and healthy environment.

Child death and injury are neither new nor the only reproductive health concerns for Palestinian or Black and Indigenous communities. We must also consider maternal death and injury due to the complications that can arise in prenatal care, pregnancy, labor, childbirth, and the postpartum. Reproductive health care includes access to safe means of birth control and abortion, and the health and well-being of newborns, adequate birth weights for neonates, and freedom from disease for infants and young children at least through the first year of their lives. In this recounting we have not even touched on the reproductive health consequences of detention and incarceration, forced removals from residential areas, limits to movement impacting access to health care, separation from family members during pregnancy, birth, and postpartum, enforced and involuntary sterilizations, and missing and murdered Indigenous women. The framework of reproductive justice and freedom from reproductive oppression indicates that Black, Indigenous and Palestinian women and their families do not enjoy the right to health and safety; instead, they continue to live within systems of extreme reproductive injustice.

Stark racial disparities in maternal and infant health in the US have persisted for decades despite continued advancements in medical care. Infants born to Black women are over twice as likely to die relative to those born to white women. Black and Indigenous women are more likely than white women to experience risk factors that contribute to infant mortality and can have long term consequences for the physical and cognitive health of children. Black and American Indian/Alaska Native women have higher rates of pregnancy related death compared to white women – greater than three or more than two times higher, respectively.[10] Black women die from complications of pregnancy at a rate of 3.55 times higher than white women and are five times more likely to be diagnosed with preeclampsia, eclampsia, and postpartum cardiomyopathy - among the leading causes for pregnancy related deaths.[11] Danya Qato reminds us:

> It is not race but racism, settler colonialism, and racial capitalism that overdetermine adverse health outcomes in the US context, especially for Black, Brown, and Indigenous people. ...which has rendered certain lives and certain neighborhoods as worthy of investment and others as disposable.

Critical concerns of reproductive injustice are around access to care, safety, and bodily autonomy in Palestine and in the US. These issues are intensified by continued exposure to systemic racism within the health care system and compounded by disproportionately high rates of incarceration for Black, Indigenous, and Palestinian women. The most recent conflict in Gaza has seen the deaths of 84,000 Palestinians, and the wounded number more than 77,000, more than 70 percent of whom are women and children. The health care system in Gaza, already under siege from the economic and political blockades, has been decimated: 26 hospitals have been destroyed, 400 heath care workers have been killed, and thousands of children have been condemned to malnutrition and famine through Israel's blocking of humanitarian aid and the targeting of aid workers.13 Gale and Kirk describe the situation for Palestinian women:

> Does a Palestinian woman really have the full right to birth and parent a child when her baby is determined a threat from birth, her womb aiding and abetting the enemy? If her maternity ward is destroyed by bombs and her doctor shot by IDF soldiers? If a settler can attack her pregnant body without repercussion, if an Israeli border police officer can shoot tear gas in her direction, if an Israeli soldier can stop her bus and force her to give birth at a military checkpoint?

On 11 January 2024, the South African legal team presented their arguments in front of the International Court of Justice for charging the State of Israel with the crime of genocide. The Republic of South Africa's High Court advocate, Adila Hassim, drew the court's attention "to the devastating generational and gendered impacts of Israel's targeted decimation of the health sector. She pointed to the denial of essential medical care and kits for the nearly 200 women delivering babies each day, all calculated to prevent Palestinian births and effectively disrupt social and biological reproduction." Nada Elia describes the deliberate nature of such actions:

> Racist population control relies specifically on violence against women. ... Israeli lawmaker Ayelet Shaked did not attempt to present the murder of Palestinian children and their mothers as unfortunate, disproportionate "collateral damage" — she openly called (in 2014) for it by asserting that Palestinian women must be killed too, because they give birth to "little snakes."[16]

In this description of only some of the reproductive injustices facing Black, Indigenous American, and Palestinian families we are not attempting to conflate or flatten the challenges for reproductive health justice across these communities - their struggles are not the same. These reproductive injustices are a feature of setter colonial oppression, and aspects of the fight for reproductive justice are quite similar across different communities. What is interesting to this discussion, moreover, is the matter of encouraging coalition building and solidarity among these peoples. We seek to obtain a deeper understanding of the specific nuances of oppressive regimes while acknowledging the general patterns of oppression for the goal of dismantling that oppression. Similarities can also be seen in the reactions of the settler colonial white supremacist state when oppressed groups rise up to take action against injustice. Marc Lamont Hill reminds us:

> With regard to Black-Palestinian solidarity, we must not only focus on the shared experiences of white supremacy and settler colonialism but also the distinctive features of life under Israeli occupation that give the Palestinian struggle its distinctive character. ... understanding and acknowledging difference enables us to engage in deeper forms of solidarity work.[17]

As well, the relationships between race and settler colonialism or Indigeneity and settler colonialism are complex and deserve to be further understood, but an in-depth explanation is beyond the scope of this essay. The racialization of Blacks or Indigenous peoples in North America is different from the racialization of Arabs and Palestinians in the Middle East and Palestine. Indigeneity is differently constituted and understood in North America and in Palestine. However, what remains is ultimately, as Erakat and Hill tell us, "a growing body of scholarship concerned with the relationship between settler colonialism and anti-Black racism as ontological frameworks as well as co-constitutive structures."[18]

As in all cases of white supremacist settler colonial states, the creation of both the US and Israel were the result of public, private, religious, military partnerships in territorial, cultural, spiritual, and economic conquest. For these reasons, it is important to recognize the long history of Black and Palestinian solidarity and to encourage strengthening of the bonds of resistance and resilience when these two global diasporas are viewed together. As Angela Davis, one of many important advocates of this solidarity since the 1960s, has said, "The tendency has been to consider Palestine a separate—and unfortunately too often marginal— issue. This is precisely the moment to encourage everyone who believes in equality and justice to join the call for a free Palestine."[19]

One of the five acts of genocide, as defined by the UN 1948 convention, describes imposing measures intended to prevent births within a targeted group. Reproductive health injustice is an indicator of genocide and a form of gendered violence as a logical process of settler colonialism; gendered violence is one role of the colonial project. The violence of settler colonialism has as its explicit goal the disappearance and elimination of Indigenous presence. The female body is specifically connected to land, kinship, sovereignty, and the possibility of alternative Indigenous futures and is, therefore, targeted for reproductive injustice. For both the US and Israel these attacks on the reproductive rights of Black, Indigenous, and Palestinian women are designed to separate their communities from their land, and to defeat and dismantle any possibility of liberation by affecting the outlook for all their children.

To imagine alternative futures, we must focus on the continued resistance and resilience of these communities in the face of oppressive state violence, surveillance, and repression. Imagining decolonial possibilities and decolonial futures is a critical step in elimination and eventual repair of the structures that currently allow reproductive injustice to continue. A key to these imagined futures is to claim a reproductive justice framework that fosters sovereignty, self-determination, and Black, Indigenous and Palestinian people's rights to live in safety and with hope.

Notes

1. Mehran Kamrava, *The Modern Middle East.*

2. Mourid Barghouti, *I Saw Ramallah.*

3. Lila Abu-Lughod, "A Feminism That Embraces Humanity."

4. Kamrava, *The Modern Middle East.*

5. Kamrava, *The Modern Middle East.*

6. Kamrava, *The Modern Middle East.*

7. Arwa Mahdawi, "Opposing oppression is a feminist act."

8. Lughod, "Feminism."

9. Lucy Truschel and Cristina Novoa, "American Indian and Alaska Native Maternal and Infant Mortality;" Linda Villarosa, "Why America's Black Mothers and Babies are in a Life-or-Death Crisis."

10. Bethany Golden, et al., "Emerging approaches to redressing multi-level racism and reproductive health disparities."

11. Danya M. Qato, "Introduction to Public Health and the Promise of Palestine;" David Williams and Chiquita Collins, "Racial Residential Segregation."

12. Omar Jabary Salamanca, et al., "It's Been 164 Days and a Long Century."

13. Leanne Gale and Gabi Kirk, "Why the Occupation Is a Reproductive Justice Issue."

14. Salamanca, et. al., "It's Been 164 Days."

15. Nada Elia, "Ending Zionism Is a Feminist Issue."

16. Marc Lamont Hill, "From Ferguson to Palestine," 954.

17. Noura Erakat and Marc Lamont Hill, "Black-Palestinian Transnational Solidarity," 14.

18. Erakat and Hill, "Black-Palestinian Transnational Solidarity," 14.

19. Angela Davis, *Freedom Is a Constant Struggle*.

References

Abu-Lughod, Lila. "A Feminism That Embraces Humanity." *In the Moment*, December 12, 2023.

Barghouti, Mourid. *I Saw Ramallah*. American University in Cairo Press, 2003.

Davis, Angela. *Freedom Is a Constant Struggle: Ferguson, Palestine, and the Foundations of a Movement*. Haymarket, 2016.

Elia, Nada. "Ending Zionism is a Feminist Issue." *The Electronic Intifada*, July 24, 2014.

Erakat, Noura, and Marc Lamont Hill. "Black-Palestinian Transnational Solidarity: Renewals, Returns, and Practice." *Journal of Palestine Studies* 48, no. 4 (Summer 2019): 7-16.

Gale, Leanne, and Gabi Kirk. "Why the Occupation is Reproductive Justice Issue." *All That's Write*, July 2, 2015.

Golden, Bethany, et al. "Emerging Approaches to Redressing Multi-Level Racism and Reproductive Health Disparities." *NPJ Digital Medicine* 5, no. 169 (2022): 1-4.

Hill, Marc Lamont. "From Ferguson to Palestine." *Biography* 41, no. 4 (Fall 2018): 942-957.

Jordan, June. *Some of Us Did Not Die: New and Selected Essays*. Civitas, 2003.

Kamrava, Mehran. *The Modern Middle East: A Political History Since the First World War*. University of California Press, 2011.

Mahdawi, Arwa. "Opposing Oppression Is a Feminist Act – *Don't Look Away from Gaza*." The Guardian, March 9, 2024.

Qato, Danya M. "Introduction: Public Health and the Promise of Palestine." *Journal of Palestine Studies* 49, no. 4 (Summer 2020): 8-26.

Salamanca, Omar Jabary, Punam Khosla, and Natasha Aruri, "It's Been 164 Days and a Long Century: Notes on Genocide, Solidarity, and Liberation." *Antipode: A Radical Journal of Geography*, April 11, 2024.

Truschel, Lucy, and Cristina Novoa. "American Indian and Alaska Native Maternal and Infant Mortality: Challenges and Opportunities." Center for American Progress, July 9, 2018.

Villarosa, Linda. "Why America's Black Mothers and Babies Are in a Life-or-Death Crisis." *New York Times Magazine*, April 11, 2018.

Williams, David, and Chiquita Collins. "Racial Residential Segregation: A Fundamental Cause of Racial Disparities in Health." *Public Health Reports* 116 (2001): 404–416.

Other References

Abdulhadi, Rabab Ibrahim. "Framing Resistance Call and Response: Reading Assata Shakur's Black Revolutionary Radicalism in Palestine," *WSQ: Women's Studies Quarterly* 46, nos. 3&4 (Fall/ Winter 2018): 226-231.

Abu-Lughod, Lila. "Imagining Palestine's Alter-Natives: Settler Colonialism and Museum Politics." *Critical Inquiry* 47, no. 1 (Autumn 2020)

Alderson, Priscilla. "Women and Children First?" *Conference on Feminism and the Politics of Childhood: Friends or Foes?* University College of London Institute of Education. November 16, 2015.

Black Women Radicals, "Toni Morrison on Palestine: "A Letter from 18 Writers."" *The Nation*, August 18, 2006.

Francis, Sahar. "Gendered Violence in Israeli Detention." *Journal of Palestine Studies* 46, no. 4 (2017): 46-61.

Moore, Darnell L. "The Occupation Stole My Words, June Jordan Helped Me to Relocate Them." *The Feminist Wire*, March 1, 2012.

Rocha, Annabel. "This Is Why What's Happening in Gaza Is a Reproductive Justice Issue Too." *The Reckon Report*, October 18, 2023.

Sister Song, Reproductive Justice. *Sister Song, Women of Color Reproductive Justice Collective*, 1994.

Thomas, James R. "The Intersection of Palestine with Ferguson, Missouri," *Journal of Ecumenical Studies* 55, no. 1 (Winter 2020): 82-90.

Wolfe, Patrick. "Settler Colonialism and the Elimination of the Native." *Journal of Genocide Research* 8, no. 4 (2006): 387–409.

'The Memories Cannot Be Brought Back': Implications of the Destruction of Libraries and Archives on Young People in Wartime Gaza

Tracie D. Hall

In November 2023, the *Washington Post* observed, "Amid the bombed-out buildings and thousands of dead in Gaza City, there is another often overlooked casualty: the embattled enclave's shattered cultural institutions, particularly its few libraries" (El Chamaa, 2023). Less than eight weeks after the start of the conflict on October 7, 2023, both the Gaza Municipal Library and the Diana Tamari Sabbagh Library along with the Rashad al-Shawa Cultural Center which housed it were completely destroyed by bombing. Israel's ongoing counter assault on Palestine comes in response to a Harakat al-Muqawama al-Islamiya (HAMAS) attack on southern Israel that killed nearly 1,200 people with over 200 more taken as hostages (Livni and Gupta, 2023). To date, Israel's retaliation has claimed the lives of nearly 14,000 people in the Gaza Strip and forcibly displaced at least 85 percent of its 1.9 million inhabitants (Abrams and Nazzal, 2023). In a statement, Gaza authorities claimed that "occupation planes targeted and turned the public library building into rubble and destroyed thousands of books, titles and documents recording the city's history and development, as well as the destruction of the library's language courses hall and other library facilities" and called the strikes, which also destroyed the municipal printing press, an attempt "to spread a state of ignorance in society" (El Chamaa, 2023).

Established in 1999 with funding from the World Bank, the Gaza Municipal Library's holdings included rare historical documents; more than 10,000 works in Arabic, English and French; and a children's library before its bombing on November 27, 2023. The Diana Tamari Sabbagh Library housed over 100,000 volumes and had sheltered displaced Palestinians before its November 25, 2023, destruction by Israel shelling. Both libraries were remembered as convening spaces for intellectuals, families, and students (El Chamaa, 2023). Raising visibility of the targeting of Gaza's libraries to the broader community, the *Literary Hub*, an online digest of the US small and independent press community, lamented, "As was the case in Sarajevo in 1992---when Bosnian Serb forces, stationed in the hills above the city, razed the National and University Library of Bosnia and Herzegovina to the ground---the targeted destruction of

Gaza's primary public library is a stark reminder that genocide is about more than just the premeditated mass extinguishing of human life; it's also about the calculated, and often vindictive, destruction of a people's culture, language, history, and shared sites of community" (Sheehan, 2023). In direct response to the libraries' decimation, the United Nations Educational, Scientific and Cultural Organization (UNESCO) noted that "cultural sites are civilian infrastructure that cannot be targeted and cannot be used as military sites," commenting further that it was "deeply concerned about the adverse impact that fighting could have on any cultural heritage in Palestine and Israel, which comes in addition to UNESCO's concerns before the ongoing fighting about the state of conservation of sites in Gaza due to the lack of local public policies on heritage and culture" (El Chamaa, 2023). Gazan scholar and library user Abdalhadi Alijla, in acknowledging that libraries play cultural roles that transcend brick and mortar buildings and physical collections, lamented that though the materiality could be replaced the library would "be missed by female students who used it as a safe place," adding "we also lost a place of gathering. The memories cannot be brought back" (El Chamaa, 2023).

Just days after the bombing of two of Gaza's major libraries, an Israeli bombardment destroyed the Central Archives of Gaza City which according to authorities contained thousands of historical documents dating back more than 150 years (Majed, 2003). Yahya al Sarraj, the head of Gaza municipality, observed, "These documents represent an integral part of our history and culture. Targeting the Central Archives poses a great danger to the city, as it contains thousands of historically valuable documents for the community." According to al Sarraj, "The Central Archives contains plans for ancient buildings of historical value and documents in the handwriting of well-known national figures," adding, "These documents, dating back a long time, were burned, turning them into ashes, erasing a large part of our Palestinian memory" (*TRT World,* 2003). By January 2024, the number of libraries and archives devastated or irreparably damaged by Israeli assaults had grown to thirteen including the Omari Mosque and Library, built in the 7th century containing collections of rare books dating back to the 14th century, and the Al-Israa University Library and National Museum, which contained over 3,000 archeological artifacts and is claimed to have been looted before being leveled by controlled detonation by the Israeli military. Libraries and archives are among the over 200 sites of historical significance hit in Israeli air raids since the start of the war in Gaza (Saber, 2024).

Compromised by years of siege, Palestine's library ecosystem had long been fragile. Prior to October 7, a 2010 survey by the Palestinian

Central Bureau of Statistics identified 13 public libraries operating in the Gaza Strip altogether, most of them ill-equipped according to poet and journalist Mosab Abu Toha's first-hand witness. Abu Toha founded the Edward Said Library, Palestine's first English-language public library, in 2017, opening a second branch in Gaza City in 2019. Abu Toha has pointed out that "Gazans face an uphill battle in importing books into the enclave, as shipments cannot go straight to Gaza---which is blockaded by Israel and Egypt---and are instead delivered to the West Bank" (El Chamaa, 2023). Detained on November 19, 2023, by Israel Defense Forces while attempting to evacuate from the Gaza Strip with his family and now an asylee separated from the libraries he founded, Abu Toha continues to advocate for the Edward Said Library and to raise awareness of the plight of libraries across Palestine (MacLaughlin, 2023).

Growing awareness of the intensive and allegedly intentional annihilation of Gaza's libraries, archives, and cultural heritage institutions has sparked charges of cultural genocide or "culturecide" against the Israeli government from the global community. Writing for *Sada*, an online journal of the Carnegie Endowment for International Peace Middle East Program, researcher Mariah Shah asserts, "What's happening in Gaza is a multi-layered act that extends far beyond the physical destruction of artifacts or the killing of individuals. These actions are part of broader destructive processes that undermine a community's heritage, identity, and existence—with profound symbolic and psychological implications for Palestinians not only in Gaza but globally" (Shah, 2024).

Indeed, among the charges brought before the United Nations' highest court, the International Court of Justice, in South Africa's genocide case against Israel in January 2024, was that "Israel has damaged and destroyed numerous centres of Palestinian learning and culture" including libraries, archives, universities, and sites of religious and historical importance. Responding to the 300 mines the Israel Defense Forces used to flatten Israa University, Chris Hazzard, an Irish member of Britain's Parliament, exclaimed on social media, "This is not self-defense. This is not counter-insurgency. This is ethnic-cleansing." (Hazzard, 2024) To be sure, the targeting and destruction of libraries, educational, and cultural heritage institutions in Palestine with the specific and lasting impact of those actions on young people is not a new tactic in the Israeli-Palestinian conflict. In two consecutive attacks, the first on July 14 and the second on July 28, 2014, a children's library established six years earlier by the International Board on Books for Young People (IBBY) in the city of Beit Hanoun located on the northeast edge of the Gaza strip near the Israeli border, was partially, then wholly destroyed by Israeli Occupation forces (IBBY, 2021). In a 2017 "Appeal for Gaza," the organization reflected,

"Ten years have passed since the IBBY libraries were set up in Gaza. Since then, life in Gaza has not improved and in many cases, it has got[ten] worse... The war on Gaza, the long years of occupation and the ongoing siege have together produced a horrific situation that demands urgent action from the local and international humanitarian organizations. The children of Gaza are victims of serious violations of their rights as a result of the ongoing humanitarian catastrophe there" (IBBY, 2017).

To be sure, the deliberate targeting of libraries during wartime has precedent. The destruction of the ancient libraries of Alexandria and Constantinople and the first iteration of the Library of Congress during the American Revolutionary War were either intentional or the result of collateral damage. During WWI, the burning and looting of Belgium's five-centuries-old library of Leuven with its 300,000 volumes by the Germans were seen as "cultural atrocities" and an act of "barbarity" by the international community (Walton, 2022). Following Hitler's adage, "No nation lives longer than the material testimony to its culture" (*Bibliotek Narodowa*, 2022), Nazis intentionally eviscerated important libraries from Serbia to Poland in an effort to reduce the impact of "Jewish intellectualism" and promote pro-German ideology. In the latter, school and university libraries were ruthlessly gutted resulting in the loss of 80% of all school libraries, and three-quarters of all scientific libraries in the country (Hench, 2010). Historian Alodia Kawecka-Gryczowa wrote of the period, "Poland...was to become a reservoir of ignorant labour, so a book or any instrument of education or science was useless – and cultural items were considered almost harmful. Therefore, school and other educational libraries were ruthlessly burned down or flooded, or their collections pulped" (*Bibliotek Narodowa*, 2022). In contemporary conflicts libraries and archives have remained primary targets of pillaging. As reported by UNESCO, "During the night of 25 August 1992, the National and University Library of Bosnia and Herzegovina, in Sarajevo, was intentionally destroyed by gunners occupying the hills surrounding the city. The fire ignited by grenades completely destroyed the historical library building and most of its collections of about 2 million volumes" (Loncarevic and Mann, 1994). The US is charged with standing by when the Baghdad National Library was ransacked in 2003, losing 60% of its archival materials and a significant portion of its rare books and documents (Moustafa, 2023). Al-Qaida was charged with the burning and theft of thousands of ancient Timbuktu manuscripts covering a range of disciplines from astronomy to theology, some dating back to the 12th century, during its raid of the historic Malian center of culture. In implementing Sharia law, the militants were said to have "banned anything considered sinful, like the manuscripts, which were seen as pagan writings" (Villamizar, 2018).

The 1954 Hague Convention for the Protection of Cultural Property in the Event of Armed Conflict held under the auspices of UNESCO produced the first international treaty to seek to pre-establish protections for "cultural property" which it defined as:

a) movable or immovable property of great importance to the cultural heritage of every people, such as monuments of architecture, art or history, whether religious or secular; archaeological sites; groups of buildings which, as a whole, are of historical or artistic interest; works of art; manuscripts, books and other objects of artistic, historical or archaeological interest; as well as scientific collections and important collections of books or archives or of reproductions of the property defined above;

(b) buildings whose main and effective purpose is to preserve or exhibit the movable cultural property defined in sub-paragraph such as museums, large libraries and depositories of archives, and refuges intended to shelter, in the event of armed conflict, the movable cultural property defined in subparagraph (a); or

(c) centres containing a large amount of cultural property as defined in sub-paragraphs (a) and (b) to be known as "centres containing monuments" (UNESCO, 1954).

As of July 2021, it has been ratified by 133 states, Israel among them.

Influenced greatly by the impact of wars as well as natural and manmade disasters on children, the United Nations subsequently convened stakeholders to draft the 1959 Declaration of the Rights of the Child. Principle 7 of that document speaks to the necessity of culturally reflective education, maintaining, "The child is entitled to receive education, which shall be free and compulsory, at least in the elementary stages. He shall be given an education which will promote his general culture and enable him, on a basis of equal opportunity, to develop his abilities, his individual judgement, and his sense of moral and social responsibility, and to become a useful member of society." In 1989, a convention was held to update and strengthen the ability of the 1959 document to protect young people. Article 17 calls out the critical function that access to mass media, information, and materials from diverse sources plays in the psycho-social, spiritual, and moral development of children and entreats state parties to, among other actions:

(a) Encourage the mass media to disseminate information and material of social and cultural benefit to the child...;

(b) Encourage international co-operation in the production,

exchange and dissemination of such information and material from a diversity of cultural, national and international sources;

(c) Encourage the production and dissemination of children's books; and

(d) Encourage the mass media to have particular regard to the linguistic needs of the child who belongs to a minority group or who is indigenous. (United Nations, 1989)

These global agreements acknowledge and codify the indispensable role that libraries and archives play in the development and maintenance of cultural memory and the irrevocable civil liberty that makes their access the right of every child. Without access to a wide and diverse body of information, young people are less equipped to meaningfully participate in, let alone contribute, to society. While the vanquisher may relish that incapacity at first, it will with time become a liability.

In ignoring the shared diplomatic regard of libraries, archives, and their irreplaceable contents as cultural infrastructure protected by humanitarian law from use as military targets, Israel -- an otherwise staunch advocate for the essential role of memory in the formation of identity -- reneges on its established agreements with the United Nations Hague Convention and Declaration on the Rights of the Child and violates the right of protected and continuous access to culturally relevant and culturally specific information guaranteed to children.

References

Abrams, R. and Nazzal, R. (2023. December 28). Israel-Hamas War: Israeli Military Admits Fault in 2 Deadly Strikes in Central Gaza. https://www. nytimes. com/live/2023/12/28/world/israel-hamas-war-gaza-news

Aljazeera. (2023, December 4). Telecommunications, internet down in Gaza as Israeli strikes intensify. Aljazeera and News Agencies. https:// www.aljazeera. com/amp/news/2023/12/4/telecommunications-internet-down-in-gaza-as-israeli-strikes-intensify

Bibliotek Narodowa. (2022, September 2). The decimation of Polish Libraries in the Second World War. https://www.bn.org.pl/en/news/4695- the-decimation-of-polish-libraries-in-the-second-world-war.html

El Chamaa, M. (2023, November 30). Gazans mourn loss of their libraries: Cultural beacons and communal spaces. *The Washington Post.* https:// www. washingtonpost.com/world/2023/11/30/gaza-library-palestinian- culture/

Hazzard, C. (2024, January 18). @ChrisHazzardSF. X. https://twitter.com/ ChrisHazzardSF/status/1747867354812301334

Hench, J. (2010) *Books as weapons*. New York: Cornell University Press.

International Board on Books for Young People – IBBY. (2021). IBBY Children in Crisis Fund. https://www.ibby.org/awards-activities/ibby- children-in-crisis-fund

International Board on Books for Young People – IBBY. (2017). IBBY Children in Crisis Fund. https://www.ibby.org/index.php?id=853

Livni, E. and Gupta, G. (2023, November 20). What we know about the war between Israel and Hamas *The New York Times*. https://www.nytimes. com/article/israel-gaza-hamas-what-we-know.html

Loncarevic, N. and Mann, C. (1994). The National and University Library of Bosnia and Herzegovina. UNESCO TV Documentary. https://www. unesco.org/archives/multimedia/document-215-eng-2

MacLaughlin, N. (2023, December 28). Virtual fundraiser to support Edward Said Libraries in Gaza. *Boston Globe*. https://www.bostonglobe. com/2023/12/28/arts/virtual-fundraiser-support-edward-said- libraries-gaza-poetry-hotline-offers-inspiration-connection-via-phone- local-booksellers-receive-funds-author-james-pattersons-bonus- program/

Majed, M. (2023, November 23). Israel destroyed Central Archives of Gaza City': Head of Gaza municipality. Anadolu Ajansı. https://www.aa.com.tr/ en/middle-east/-israel-destroyed-central-archives-of-gaza-city-head- of-gaza-municipality/3068555

Moustafa, L. (2023, December 12). When libraries like Gaza's are destroyed, what's lost is far more than books. *Los Angeles Times*. https:// www.latimes.com/opinion/story/2023-12-12/gaza-library-bombing

Saber, I.F. (2024, January 14). A 'cultural genocide': Which of Gaza's heritage sites have been destroyed? *Aljazeera*. https://www.aljazeera.com/news/2024/1/14/a-cultural-genocide-which-of-gazas-heritage-sites- have-been-destroyed

Shah, M. (2024, February 8). Vanishing Ink: Palestinian culture under threat in Gaza. Carnegie Endowment for International Peace. https:// carnegieendowment.org/sada/91577

Sheehan, D. (2023, November 27). Gaza's main public library has been destroyed by Israeli bombing. *Literary Hub*. https://lithub.com/gazas- main-public-library-has-been-destroyed/

TRT World (2023, December 3). 'Israel attempts to erase Palestinian memory':

Gaza municipality. https://www.trtworld.com/middle-east/israel-attempts-to-erase-palestinian-memory-gaza-municipality-16033342

UNESCO. (1954, May 14). Convention for the Protection of Cultural Property in the Event of Armed Conflict with Regulations for the Execution of the Convention. The United Nations Educational, Scientific and Cultural Organization. https://www.unesco.org/en/legal-affairs/ convention-protection-cultural-property-event-armed-conflict- regulations-execution-convention

United Nations. (2023, September 21). Human Rights Council Continues General Debate on the Promotion and Protection of All Human Rights, Civil, Political, Economic, Social and Cultural Rights, Including the Right to Development. United Nations Human Rights Council. https://www. article19.org/ data/files/Internet_Statement_Adopted.pdf.

United Nations. (1989, November 20). Convention on the Rights of the Child. United Nations General Assembly resolution. https://www.ohchr. org/en/ instruments-mechanisms/instruments/convention-rights-child

Villamizar, M. (2018, June 27). Preserving the priceless manuscripts of Timbuktu. Public Broadcasting Chanel. https://www.pbs.org/newshour/ show/ preserving-the-priceless-manuscripts-of-timbuktu

Walton, D. (2022, September 25). When the University of Leuven library was burnt down – twice! Discovering Belgium. https://www. discoveringbelgium. com/leuven-university-library/

The Sin of Neutrality or
The Tail of the Mouse
Talib Kweli

"If you are neutral in situations of injustice, you have chosen the side of the oppressor. If an elephant has its foot on the tail of a mouse and you say that you are neutral, the mouse will not appreciate your neutrality."
- Desmond Tutu

In 2020, a ten-year-old Palestinian MC named MC Abdul went viral with his own rendition of Wiz Khalifa's global smash hit "See You Again." At an age when many kids around the world are playing video games or team sports, Abdul was making videos of himself spitting lyrics about life and loss in Palestine while walking around the bombed buildings of war-torn Gaza, a place where his family had been trapped since his grandparents were coerced into leaving their homes and becoming refugees during the foundation of the Israeli state in 1948. By 2022, MC Abdul was 13 years old and began to hold a special place in my heart when he repurposed the Black Star song "Respiration" to show us what life is like in Palestine through a child's eyes. With a dimly lit street corner in Gaza as his backdrop, this child recorded a video of himself spitting bars like –

> Twenty four seven I'll be fighting those demons, every year another war with another season, see my people die got my heart really bleeding…

On our album *Mos Def and Talib Kweli Are Black Star*, 1998, Yasiin Bey rhymed about how his "raps hold a gat to your back like Palestinians." In 2002, on my debut solo album, *Quality*, I rapped about how "Israelis got tanks and Palestinians got rocks." Lyrically I have been supporting a free Palestine for over 20 years, so to witness the evolution of a Palestinian MC who was inspired by my lyrics was very special for me. By the time he turned 15, MC Abdul's family was able to relocate to America, but they are the exception to the rule. Most never make it out, and in every war, the children are the most vulnerable. The youngest of us are the least able to deal with the hunger and disease that comes with facing the business end of one of the world's biggest guns.

According to Dr. Iman Farajallah, in her article titled "The Invisible Wounds of Palestinian Children," Palestinian children experience complex continuous trauma (CCT) due to living in an environment rife with poverty, war, famine, lack of infrastructure, the destruction of homes, and the loss of loved ones. The continued bombing of Gaza contributes to a lack of the most basic needs like clean water and electricity. According to a 2022 report called *Trapped* by Save The Children, 95% of Palestinian children experience mental health challenges, over half have considered suicide, and three out of five Palestinian children engage in self-harm.

Back in 2014 I was offered ten times my normal rate to play an Israeli music festival. I jumped at the opportunity. When I announced the show, the disappointment from my fan base came as swiftly as I took the gig. It turns out that I had developed a fan base that expected a higher than average level of awareness from me when it came to movement work. While I considered myself to be pro-Palestine, I certainly didn't see myself as "anti-Jewish." So why wouldn't I perform in Israel? I argued this point on social media with fans who were disappointed in my choice. I told them of my plans to invite Palestinian activists on stage and how I would contribute money to pro-Palestinian causes and I would also do a free show in Palestine during my trip to the region. None of this mattered to my challengers. They simply wanted me to respect the boycott of Israel.

I knew I didn't agree with the way the Israeli government treated not just Palestinians but people of color in general, but I was unaware of the boycott of Israel led by the BDS Movement. I didn't reconsider my position until members of the pioneering Palestinian hip hop group DAM got in touch with me and, after explaining to me how much they loved my music, asked me to not perform in Israel. If the Palestinians who love my music are asking me to stand in solidarity with them and respect the boycott, who was I to stand against them?

Julius Caesar once said, "it's only hubris if I fail." It was certainly pride that led me to believe that I could use my art to "heal the divide" between Israel and Palestine. How can one heal a wound that is constantly being reopened? The members of DAM explained to me how BDS was a peaceful solution to the conflict in the region. As someone who is anti-war, this appealed to me. BDS stands for boycott, divest and sanctions, and as a child of parents who participated in the anti-apartheid movement against the government of South Africa during the 1980s, I understood the assignment. I canceled my Israeli performance and announced that I stood in solidarity with the BDS Movement.

When I used to be on social media, I engaged a lot, which meant I was excessively trolled by some of the most deplorable groups of people our society has to offer. With that said, the Zionist trolls were at once the most violent and most dedicated of the bunch. When pro-BDS folks were coming for me online, they were largely expressing a deep disappointment. A handful of them were rude, but for the most part the engagement was respectful even in disagreement. Comparatively, the Zionist trolls were out for blood. There was a bunch of name calling, racism, and some threats thrown in for good measure. At one point, I asked one of the Zionist trolls who had been posting disrespectful comments on my page every two minutes for two days straight how he was able to keep up such a relentless pace, and he responded that he was one of many people assigned to troll my account. "This is my shift," was his initial response.

In 2019, the German parliament condemned the BDS movement as anti-Semitic. While it's hard for me to see Germany as an authority on what constitutes anti-Semitism, this motion had a real effect on my career. At the time I was gearing up for a month-long German tour that was set to roll until Zionist accounts began to troll the German venues I was scheduled to appear at and began complaining about how I was a supporter of BDS and, therefore, anti-Semitic. One by one, German venues across the country began to demand that I denounce BDS. I saw being asked to denounce the peaceful BDS Movement as anti-free speech, and I refused to, which led to the cancellation of my tour and a loss of revenue.

As hate crimes against Jewish people continue to rise I will continue to stand in solidarity with Jewish communities against all anti-Jewish ideology and action. I also continue to support a free Palestine, and I always will. These are not mutually exclusive concepts. The deadly attack on southern Israel by armed Palestinian groups on October 7, 2023, that resulted in the killing of 1,200 people was without a doubt horrific. However, when you consider the fact that according to the United Nations over one million children have been uprooted from their homes and over 13,000 children have been killed in Gaza as victims of Israel's response to the October 7 attack, it feels like an understatement to call that an overcorrection.

There is a lot of media attention surrounding the 242 Israeli hostages who were initially taken by Hamas and rightfully so. Taking hostages is a war crime. Receiving far less attention are the almost 7,000 Palestinians who Israel has currently detained and who have never been charged with a crime or received any due process. These Palestinian detainees, who often report that they are being tortured by the Israeli military, include political activists, human rights defenders, and children. According to the Israeli human rights organization HaMoked, scores of Palestinian children are currently detained in Israel without charge or trial. According to the Children's Defense Fund International, Israel detains 500-700 Palestinian children a year. How are they not considered hostages? Why is there seemingly no value placed on their lives? No child, Israeli or Palestinian, should be used as a bargaining chip during a war.

From where I sit, it's extremely dishonest to start any analysis of this conflict with the tragic events of October 7, 2023. Doing so erases decades of Palestinian struggle, oppression, and death at the hands of Israel. This conflict is not about Muslims vs Jews; its about colonialism vs anti-colonialism. Due to Israel's colonial mentality, doctors are left stunned when they visit hospitals in Gaza. As of this writing, only about a dozen of Gaza's 36 hospitals are functional at all, and the majority of its intensive care beds are occupied by wounded children clinging to life. When it's the children who remain the most affected by the violence, it's easy to pick a side.

In September 2017, journalist Nathan J. Robinson wrote an article called "A Quick Reminder of Why Colonialism Was Bad" for *Current Affairs* in which he argued that "downplaying colonial atrocities is the moral equivalent of Holocaust denial." Because of the settler colonialism of Israel, Gaza is the deadliest place for civilians and aid workers in the world in the year 2024. According to the *Encyclopedia Britannica,* Zionism is "a Jewish nationalist movement that has as its goal the creation and support of a Jewish national state in Palestine." In Rashid Khalidi's book, *The Hundred Years' War on Palestine, A History of Settler Colonialism and Resistance,* Khalidi writes about Ze'ev Jabotinsky, a Zionist leader and founder of the Jewish Self-Defense Organization. In an essay called "The Iron Law" explaining how to properly colonize Palestine, Jabotinsky wrote , "If you wish to colonize a land in which people are already living, you must provide a garrison for the land or find a benefactor who will maintain the garrison… Zionism is a colonizing adventure and, therefore, its stands or falls on the question of the armed forces."

Theodore Herzl is widely regarded as the father of modern Zionism. Herzl founded the Zionist Organization and attempted to start a Jewish state by promoting Jewish immigration to Palestine. In a *Mondoweiss* article from November of 2015 titled "US and Israel Rewrite History of UN Resolution That Declared Zionism Is Racism," journalist Ben Norton writes, "In a 1902 letter to Cecil Rhodes - a diamond magnate and white supremacist British colonialist with oceans of African blood on his hands - Herzl, writing of 'the idea of Zionism, which is a colonial idea' requested help colonizing historic Palestine." "Because it is something colonial," Herzl wrote. "I want you to… put your stamp of authority on the Zionist plan." The name Cecil Rhodes should be a red flag to anyone who understands the evils of apartheid. Anyone saying that Zionist ideology is not unapologetically rooted in settler colonialism based on military violence, apartheid, and imperialism has not studied history.

Right here in our own American backyard, Black folks are still too often treated like second class citizens. With that said, our power lies in numbers, solidarity, and intersectionality. When Ferguson was ground zero for the movement due to the murder of Michael Brown by Ferguson police, I witnessed Palestinian activists on the front lines resisting right along with us. A number of activists I worked with in Ferguson were invited to Palestine shortly after and came back wiser, stronger, and more dedicated to our freedom. There is well documented solidarity between the movement for Black lives and the Palestinian movement for liberation.

"The greatest danger to a democracy is an uninformed electorate." - Thomas Avant.

Wannabe tyrants will always try to control and manipulate the flow of information. During a senate hearing on the potential banning of TikTok, Nebraska's Republican senator Pete Ricketts stated that he is in favor of the ban because pro-Palestinian content is being seen on TikTok 50 times more than pro-Israeli content. At just 15 years old, Palestinian rapper MC Abdul is a featured performer on Rolling Loud, one of music's biggest festivals. Just like in Ferguson, Occupy Wall Street, and other social justice movements I've participated in, I see young folks who identify as White and Jewish folks also supporting a free Palestine. I'd like to see way more.

My original goal for writing this chapter was to tell the story of how I got cancelled in Germany for refusing to denounce BDS, but the more I wrote, the more my true intention began to crystallize. I'm not writing this for the oppressed class; I'm writing this for the oppressor class. The onus is not on the oppressed to stop the oppression; that's a job for the oppressor. The problem is that the oppressed don't have the privilege of waiting for the oppressor to figure that out. And as always, it will be the children who lead the way.

Killing Hope
Dave Zirin

Despite all the divisions and barriers that plague the world, there is one common thread: the joy that young people feel when they play. It is a common cultural language and the international joys of play---the joys of sport---provide a precious vision of a world at peace. That is why it is so brutal when war obliterates physically safe places for children to play and kills their teammates, their friends, and their heroes. For the young people of Gaza that was the case long before October 7, 2023. Living in an open-air prison of 2.1 million people and surrounded by barbed wire, checkpoints, and the sea, had always made playing sports a precarious venture for the young. Yet, in an act of play that doubled as an act of resistance, the young of Gaza created a rich and varied sporting culture. The number of sports played in Gaza before October 7 included soccer, basketball, skateboarding, and the relative newcomer ultimate frisbee.

However, even with networks of leagues, coaches, and playing fields, there were blockades and walls that kept Gaza youth sports organizations from joining their teammates in the West Bank, not to mention greater Israel, to play in contests either local or international. Unlike youth travel teams in the rest of the world, which can broaden the horizons of the young and create lifelong memories, generations of child athletes of Gaza have been stuck in an open-air prison not of their making, unable to see the majority of their own country. This de facto prohibition of youth sports being able to flower fully is not merely a byproduct of Israeli oppression. It is central to Palestinian subjugation. When you kill the games of the young, you are killing their dreams. When you drive a stake through their dreams, you are killing hope. It is the death of normalcy, the smothering of that unique language of the young at play. It is Israel acculturating Palestinian children to feel immobilized, frustrated, and defeated.

By December 2023, at least 85 Palestinian athletes, 55 of them soccer players, had been killed in Israeli attacks. 18 were children; 37 were teenagers. There are too many stories like that of Mjahed Saaida, a 14-year-old killed in an Israeli airstrike while playing soccer with his friends. His father, Mohammad Saaida, said afterwards in shock, "I saw him and I knelt over his body, not knowing what to do. All his face was bloody, full of shrapnel—and his leg was cut off."

Another part of killing the hope of children is taking out their heroes. Hundreds of Palestinian athletes have been killed since October 7 along with team managers and office workers. Most notably, soccer star Mohammed Barakat, also known as "the legend of Khan Younis," was killed by Israeli forces. Barakat was a Palestinian national team member and the first player in the history of Gaza's Palestinian league to score 100 goals. (This is particularly remarkable when you consider that Palestinian soccer league has only been able to complete a handful of seasons since 1977 due to disruption caused by the occupation.) Before he was killed by Israeli air strikes, Barakat filmed his last public words. He said, "Perhaps life has ended, or perhaps there is still life ahead, and only the Knower of the Unseen of the heavens and the earth determines this... So I ask for your forgiveness and your prayers... My mother, my father, my children, by Allah, you are dear to me and precious to me... I entrust you to Allah, whose trust is never lost... I conclude here... your prayers... This is where I end." Another who was killed in an Israeli air strike was Palestinian Olympic soccer team CEO Hani al-Masry. The 42-year-old, known in Palestine also as Abu al-Abed, was a midfielder for the Al-Maghazi Club and then the Gaza Sports Club before retiring in 2018.

Think about what it would feel like if Israel bombed the home of LeBron James or if they sent a drone to kill Lionel Messi. The shock and outrage would reverberate across the globe not only because they would be killing a famed civilian, but because when you kill someone that children adore, you are also killing their capacity to love. It's about tearing at the desire to live.

One might think that international sporting bodies like FIFA would be up in arms over Israel's brazen killing of players and staff. After all, FIFA President Gianni Infantino, responding in 2022 to criticism of the decision to host the World Cup in Qatar, said, "Today I feel Qatari. Today I feel Arabic. Today I feel African. Today I feel gay. Today I feel disabled. Today I feel [like] a migrant worker." Clearly if there is one thing Infantino does not "feel" is Palestinian. FIFA has been silent while its member clubs in Gaza have been bombed to dust. Their only action was to send a letter of condolence to Israel after the Hamas killings on October 7. This is shameful.

The hypocrisy of FIFA is astounding. After Russia invaded Ukraine, Putin's nation was condemned and sanctioned in the harshest terms. But symbolic of the dehumanization Palestinians must endure, Israel's actions have not merited a word. As for the International Olympic Committee, another organization that sanctioned and condemned Russia, they have said little more than that any protesting of Israeli athletes at the 2024 Paris Olympics will not be tolerated.

In the past, there have been calls to ban Israel from international athletic competition due to the ways that Israeli apartheid mangled

Palestinian sports operations. The Israeli response invariably has been that they are being held to a "higher standard" than other countries also engaged in awful acts against civilians, and this higher standard is rank anti-Semitism. But how could anyone short of a zealot not see that the genocide in Gaza, the killing of Olympic players and coaches, the use of stadiums as torture camps, and the targeting of children cannot be tolerated? What is the point of having these athletic bodies, allegedly devoted to peace, if they choose silence at such a dire moment? When there was an international movement against South African apartheid, people like 1968 Olympians Tommie Smith and John Carlos protested against the country being a part of the games. That movement must be revived. To have Israel play in these events before the world would be a form of "sportswashing," where Israel gets legitimized as a part of the community of nations when it is attempting to assassinate an entire people.

Playing sports at its best is about freedom, about dreaming of achieving something greater than you thought was possible. As the great Olympian Wilma Rudolph said, "Never underestimate the power of dreams and the influence of the human spirit. The potential for greatness lives within each of us." Nothing marks the nihilism of Israel's genocidal war and ongoing occupation quite like this indisputable fact: they don't want the children of Gaza to dream. In plain fact, they don't want the children of Gaza to live.

First writing since…[1]
Zahra Ali

First writing since

> words don't mean
> anything anymore.

What are words after all? Just sounds, fragments of our feelings, of our limitations.

I wake up every morning wondering how the sun continues to rise, how we continue to write.

When a child in Gaza says that she does not want to live anymore.

Who would dare tell her not to despair, that إن مع العسر يسرا, that after hardship comes ease?[2]

I think of what she said. I think of her.

I think of the little girl growing in my womb. I think of when I was a little girl, the child of Iraqi refugees.

I have, like her, seen my motherland, Iraq, intentionally, meticulously, and with all the cruelty the world can gather, destroyed. My people, massacred, maimed.

The apocalypse.

The mass graves. Death coming from the sky. The same bombs, the same bullets, the same tanks, the same heartless public opinion.

Death, made in America.[3]

It is the same world that is now watching the live broadcast of her people, the people of Palestine, being bombed and starved to death.

The same world that found good reasons to carpet bomb Iraq and deprive Iraqis of the means to survive for over a decade.

A million of us, mostly children, were killed as a result of what they like to call the "UN sanctions." An invisible war designed by the Americans, to kill us a slow death, starving, lacking everything that sustains life.

We were then invaded, occupied, bombed, shot, arrested, tortured. The war against my people never ended. The war against the very existence of the people of Palestine is intensifying.

If for our enemies, we are not human enough, for our allies, we are a different kind of human. We are heroes, martyrs. Our supporters praise our resilience, our صمود, our steadfastness.

For our oppressors, our existence is a threat. Our supporters take pride in our suffering. They need us to be strong. Our death, not our lives, matters as long as it provides others a sense of purpose.

Despair is a right.

Like the
right to
breath.[4]

There is nothing to celebrate in survival. We were not born to be martyrs.

A child does not choose to be brave, to act like an adult.

Childhood, just like despair, is a right.

Did you hear?

A child in Gaza says that she does not want to live anymore. True, here in the US where I now live, in the heart of the empire that killed my people and hers, she is not a child, she is invisible. When an Arab child, an Arab girl, an Arab woman, is not invisible, she is at best someone to save from her own people. Our brothers, our fathers, are never given such privilege.

There are no civilians in Gaza. Nowhere is safe in Gaza.

For the Israeli, the American, the Western public opinion, an Arab man, an Arab boy, is never a victim. There are no children in Gaza, only present or future threats to eliminate.

Terrorism: highly organized crimes perpetrated by existing nation-states.

The war against our existence is never defensive. There is no self-defense in genocide. The "war on terror" is preemptive. Its objective is precisely to prevent and to erase the slightest possibility that we might take our destinies in our own hands.

Khamas is Israel's N word.

Since October, I realized that I never overcame the shock I was born into.

They did call it "Shock and Awe."

I am unable to write, to be articulate.

Nothing makes sense. Nothing feels the same.
When a child in Gaza says that she does not want to live anymore.

As a scholar of the Middle East based in an American public university, a transnational feminist, an educator, I should be busying myself writing op-eds, lecturing in teach-ins and webinars.

Haven't I spent the last two decades of my life explaining, proving, showing, that we Iraqis, Afghanis, Palestinians, are indeed people who deserve to live? Reminding Americans of what they have done to us, of what they have done to themselves?

Where did all the words go?

Silence is a question.

Since October, I cannot adopt an analytical tone. The tone taken by media commentators, political scientists, and experts, whoever they are, and whatever they are advocating for.

In the articles I stopped writing since October, I would have explained that this is the intensification of Israeli settler-colonial violence on the people of Gaza, a continuation of a genocidal campaign that started more than 75 years ago. That the process of erasure of the indigenous population in historic Palestine was always an imperial project, first the British, then the Americans made it possible. A settler colony supporting another settler colony. Imperial solidarity at its best.

In the teach-ins I didn't give, I would have said that in many ways, what is happening in Gaza today is a continuation of the "war on terror." Same lies, same racist and Islamophobic media propaganda justifying the very destruction of entire countries, the dehumanization of entire peoples. I would have also explained that just like nothing started on 9/11, nothing started on October 7th. That Iraq and Palestine were established by the British as postcolonial states in the 1920s, and that for different and intertwined political, social, and economic reasons, Iraqis and Palestinians have been considered disposable by white supremacist capitalist powers.

I would have added that their war of terror killed more than 4 million in Iraq and the region, and displaced 38 million people.

But where would these words go?

> when Americans
> still say Never Forget

When people don't matter, numbers are irrelevant.

The only numbers that matter to Americans in Iraq are the ones of the American soldiers killed in "the battlefield." Today, it is the number of Israeli hostages.

Soldiers and hostages "come back home."

> Where do we come
> back to?

To the ruins of our homes? There is no place to flee, there has never been anywhere to flee for the people of Gaza.

But everything has been said.

Only the words of the people of Gaza truly matter. Only the words of the children of Gaza. Nothing else.

Children, adolescents, and young Gazans are showing the world in real time what is happening to them. They know exactly what is happening. Children see through us.

Children are life itself in its magnificence, in its glory, and all its secrets, in all its truth.

Children in Gaza who survive genocide say that they don't want to live anymore.

I imagine myself holding the little girl, my little girl, in my arm, and whispering in her ear: "Little one. حورلا حور اي, soul of my soul, I too sometimes feel exactly like you do.[5] Let me tell you a story, my story. I come from the land of the two rivers, the rivers that once saw the start of every story. My people suffered just like your people. We lost our families, our homes, our streets. Many of us were forced to live far away from our land, from our people. We thought that we were lost, that there was nothing left for us in this world. But slowly, as time went by, we realized that despite being away from them, our martyrs, our two rivers, are still and will always be in our hearts. يتببح, my love, as long as you keep love in our hearts, you are not lost, you have not yet been defeated."

Notes

1. This title is inspired by a poem of Suheir Hammad, the author of *Born Palestinian, Born Black* (Harlem River Press, 1996) written after 9/11.

2. "Ina ma'a al-'usri yusra" can be translated from Arabic as "after hardship comes ease" is a widely known and commonly used verse from the Qur'an, Sura al-Sharh, Verse 5.

3. I choose to employ the problematic and colonial term "America" instead of United States of America because it is the term used by people in the Arab worlds to refer to this country as such, and to its people as "Americans."

4. This is inspired by the poem composed by the Egyptian political prisoners Ahmed Douma and Alaa Abd El-Fattah titled "Graffiti for Two." They composed it from their prison ward, yelling from their respective cells; it was released on the third anniversary of the Egyptian revolution, the 25th of January 2014.

5. "Ya ruh al-ruh", soul of my soul in English, is the term used by Khaled Nabhan as he bid farewell to his three-year-old granddaughter Reem killed by Israel in December 2023. Referring to loved ones as "my soul" is very common in Arabic.

There Can Be No Moral High Ground Unless We Stop War on Children
Ezra Hyland

"More have suffered than we can find were active in this bloody affair."

On a hot summer night in 1712, a group of "three and twenty" enslaved Africans got together and attempted to gain their freedom through violent insurrection. Due to his quick reaction, only "nine Christians" were killed, according to the report written by Robert Hunter, Governor of New York, to the Lords of Trade. When the insurrection was finally suppressed, 6 rebels chose death by their own hands, leaving 17 of the original 23 alive. But in court 27 were convicted, and 21 were executed: "Some were burnt, others hanged, one broke on the wheel, and one hung alive in chains in the town, so that there has been the most exemplary punishment inflicted that could be possibly thought of..." Only one of the condemned, a woman, was spared because she was pregnant. His blood lust satisfied, the Governor wrote, "more have suffered than we can find were active in this bloody affair."[1]

After patting himself on the back for his creativity in devising and executing the "exemplary punishments," he then astoundingly listed several enslaved Africans and Indians whom he felt were unjustly held or punished and asked for permission to reprieve them. As proper as it may have been for him to seek justice as he understood it, he could never figure out why the enslaved Africans did what they did. He wrote "[perhaps] they had resolved to revenge themselves, for some hard usage they apprehended to have received from their masters, for I can find no other cause."[2] His white-supremacist mind could not imagine Black people using violent means to regain the freedom taken from them by violence.

311 years later, those infected with the logic of white supremacy still seem perplexed that the abused and voiceless would violently revolt against those who had done violence to them. To be clear, the attack of October 7, 2023, was wrong, morally, tacitly, and spiritually. There is no scenario in which attacking civilians and taking hostages is justifiable. But as Martin Luther King Jr. stated more and more near the end of his time on earth, "violence is the language of the unheard." For the last 76 years many Palestinians have too often found themselves voiceless, with no real allies, and powerless except through violence.

On the other hand, no matter how unpopular the Israeli government, or how some may feel about the founding of the nation, we can never deny a people the right to self-defense or, ultimately, we deny ourselves the right to self-defense. But genocide is not self-defense. As Black people, despite our long allyship with Jewish people, we cannot let that bind our tongues to the truth of the genocidal war crimes being committed every day by the Israeli government. With the same spirit the world rose up to demand an end to police violence after the police lynching of George Floyd, Black people must scream out "Stop the Genocide in Palestine!"

The charge Genocide is not hyperbole. Genocide is an internationally recognized crime by which acts are committed with the intent to destroy, in whole or in part, a national, ethnic, racial, or religious group. These acts fall into five categories[3]:

1. Killing members of the group

2. Causing serious bodily or mental harm to members of the group

3. Deliberately inflicting on the group conditions of life calculated to bring about its physical destruction in whole or in part

4. Imposing measures intended to prevent births within the group

5. Forcibly transferring children of the group to another group

No reasonable person can doubt that at the minimum the first 3 categories of genocidal acts apply to what is happening in Palestine. The Israeli government and the IDF are also committing many other crimes that don't meet the legal definition of genocide but are no less inhumane and could be considered war crimes, crimes against humanity, ethnic cleansing, and mass killing.[5]

At the time of this writing, the IDF has killed over 14,000 "unoffending, innocent, and beautiful" children. Uncounted thousands more have been injured, have lost family members, and been driven from their homes. Over 2 million Palestinians have been displaced. These acts meet the definition of War Crimes as defined by the International Criminal Court. The targeting and killing of children continue each day. Nothing seems off limits. Even schools and hospitals are not safe.

In 1991, Israel signed the Convention on the Rights of Children (the United States and Somalia haven't ratified the convention) which identified attacks against schools or hospitals as one of its 6 grave violations against children in times of conflict. The IDF, using in many cases American weapons, have destroyed more than 390 educational institutions.[6] 98 healthcare facilities, including 27 hospitals, have been damaged. In some areas the attacks have been so unrelenting that

Palestinians can't even bury their dead. According to the Palestinian Health Ministry, stray dogs were eating the bodies of civilians in the yard of a hospital because no one was able to bury the dead amid the bombardment.[7] It is surprising that Americans who spent more than $100 billion on pet-related expenditures, vastly more than what was spent on recreational reading material, alcoholic beverages, women's clothing, homelessness, and addiction treatment,[8] haven't taken to the streets to protest the poor diet those dogs have been forced to consume.[9]

If any group other than Black people in this world should understand that the human will to survive is more powerful than any oppressor's desire to destroy, that no matter how brutal the punishment people will continue to fight for freedom, it should be the people of Israel. In the words of Dr. King, an eye for an eye and a tooth for a tooth, leaves both parties toothless and blind. But even when blind and toothless, a person can continue to live, create, and love. Israel's current policy is creating another generation of desperate people who will choose death over debasement. Each bomb, each bullet, each burned school, shattered body, and scorched soul, doesn't bring us closer to peace, but creates the next generation of bombers, shooters, and fighters, those who, in the words of James Baldwin, have nothing to lose or live for.

Notes

1. Deirdre Mullane. *Crossing The Danger Water*. Anchor Books, New York, 1993, p.21

2. Deirdre Mullane. *Crossing The Danger Water*. Anchor Books, New York, 1993, p.21

3. https://www.un.org/en/genocideprevention/genocide.shtml

4. https://www.ushmm.org/genocide-prevention/learn-about-genocide-and-other-mass-atrocities/what-is-genocide

5. There are a number of other serious, violent crimes that do not fall under the specific definition of genocide. They include crimes against humanity, war crimes, ethnic cleansing, and mass killing.

6. https://kinginstitute.stanford.edu/publications/autobiography-martin-luther-king-jr/chapter-21-death-illusions

7. https://www.npr.org/2024/01/24/1226534897/israel-has-destroyed-hundreds-of-educational-institutions-in-gaza-since-the-war#:~:text=in%20Gaza%20City.-,Israel%20has%20destroyed%20more%20than%20390%20educational%20institutions%20in%20Gaza,many%20Palestinian%20schools%20and%20universities.

8. https://www.middleeasteye.net/news/israel-palestine-gaza-war-stray-dogs-eat-bodies-wounded-face-imminent-death-besieged-gaza

9. https://www.bls.gov/opub/btn/volume-12/we-love-our-pets-and-our-spending-proves-it-1.htm#_edn2

If We Must Live: A Talk from Teachers

Sabina Vaught, T. Elon Dancy, and Christopher M. Wright

A child screams over her beloved father's shrouded body in the bombed out UNRWA school yard, as we listen to the school meeting open with a land acknowledgment that evades land back.

A mother delicately kisses her twins' martyr-cold foreheads, back-and-forth, back-and-forth, back-and-forth, as we listen to a school administrator report out on the newly funded equity project.

A father carefully moves his child's hand down with his own, before she feels the fatal hole in her head, whispers reassurances to her before she feels fear, holds her gaze as she transforms into a bird of Paradise, as teacher colleagues post joyous group selfies from a social and emotional learning conference.

A child stares at a camera through terrified eyes, peering out above the gaping absence of once chubby, kissed cheeks, above hollow and horror, her body starved by the Zionist terrorists, as we are invited to join the after-party of the school meeting for treats and eats. To gorge.

We are teachers. If teachers must be quiet and polite as Palestinian children must die, if we must be convivial and collegial as Palestinians must be slaughtered, if we must be inoffensive for the new multicultural civility, for the diverse professionalism requisite of genocide, then we should also don state military uniforms and brandish corporate weapons. We should mark notches: one, two, three, four, 80 children massacred: by department meetings and award celebrations and professional development workshops run by the deputized, included descendants of other genocides. Infant limbs scattered on the conference room table, school-child blood splattered on zoom screens, toddler entrails at the potluck buffet.

Or we should don the uniform of the resistance (as in, assume the stance), and take up arms of liberation (most centrally, the study of truth and knowledge), and refuse the state and its willing professional-class education militias. "We are in a revolutionary situation," said James Baldwin[1] to an audience of teachers over 60 years ago. We, as all teachers have been since the beginning of empire's schooling project, are in a revolution. Schooling is a centerpiece of the U.S. war project, focusing surgically, singularly on the future in the shape of children. Children, both figurative and literal, represent futures or their destruction. We are in a fight for the future of peoples. In a revolution, you are part of the resistance or you are part of the occupation. You are part of the future or part of the genocide.

As teachers, we resist within those institutions that are part of the war against children: K-12 schools and universities. But what does that mean for teachers working from the belly of the beast, the heart of genocidal empire? What are the particular conditions and strategies of a solidarity with the resistance? As teachers, we consider what it means for futures when we must live.[2]

War and the Resistance

In his will, Palestinian intellectual, activist, teacher, and writer Basel al-Araj wrote what he called the "8 rules and insights on the nature of war" in Gaza's resistance movement.[3] These were published after the IOF[4] assassinated him and have become a guiding framework for guerrilla resistance and study. We draw directly from al-Araj's 8 rules to organize our reflections on how to make sense of what teachers resisting in solidarity (or, in the resistance movement) are experiencing; how we might consider being called into solidarity; and how to reflect on possibility and purpose as we teach with the movements for the self-determined liberation of peoples everywhere.

How to Make Sense of What Teachers Resisting in Solidarity (or, in the Resistance Movement) Are Experiencing

> *Rule 1 "The Palestinian resistance consists of guerrilla formations ... War is never based on the logic of conventional wars and the defense of fixed points and borders ... So never measure it against conventional wars."*

Common sense would have us believe that conventional wars are waged between militaries, and by adults. That the genocide in Gaza is, in part, a war on children comes from a long practice of asymmetrical warfare that is a hallmark of western genocidal paradigms. Children are always targets of projects aimed at eliminating, reducing, enslaving, and occupying peoples. Why? Because they represent generations of a society, longevity of cultural knowledge and community practice, and because in fact those of us whose values lie with liberation recognize we are always children--of families, communities, movements, and peoples who raised us--and that all children are our responsibility. It is only for colonizers that children are differentiated in value and that adulthood is a forsaking of their child relations. In this way, they abandon their own foremothers, their knowledge, and their people. Indeed, colonizers understand the condition of being child-like as one of inadequacy for civilization, autonomy, or human regard.

146

As teachers who understand children as generations, how do we build resistance in guerrilla formations? First, we study schools—state institutions organized around young people. In the U.S., schools have been instruments of control and captivity: Indigenous children were kidnapped, coerced, or forced into schools run by the military and meant to both literally and culturally kill them. Schools have been sites of violent differentiation: Black children were legally excluded from schools, but then legally compelled into schools that surveil, punish, and denigrate them in a vast, synchronized effort to normalize and enshrine every form of subordination available. University disciplines and fields built and build out intractable encyclopedic truths that provide tested rationale for domination. These examples are not the exception, as narratives of "public" or "democratic" schooling would have us believe. In fact, schooling in the U.S. has been part of the nation-state's project to control people through children. As Sabina and co-authors have written elsewhere of the purpose of schools in relation to Indigenous and Black peoples in the U.S., "We understand schools ... as a function of US conquest statecraft—as part of a broad and deep war structure of coming for children."[5]

In the U.S., the largest war division is the school system. This state project extends into and emerges from universities where teachers are trained in the unnamed warfare of schooling. They are inducted into the curricula and pedagogies, the evaluation, management, and policy of an occupying, genocidal nation. Schools that prepare teachers in alignment with the state are war agencies: outposts, forts, and central command; bases, stations, and recruiting centers. Within these schools our guerrilla formations may be very small. But we are not disheartened. It is the originary function of schools as a war against children and their peoples that shapes our understanding of guerrilla formations in teaching and teacher preparation and is the context of the lessons for sustained, evident solidarity with Palestinian resistance.

> Rule 2 "The enemy will spread photos and videos of their invasion into Gaza ... This is part of the psychological warfare in guerrilla wars; you allow your enemy to move as they wish so that they fall into your trap and you strike them. You determine the location and timing of the battle. So you may see photos [of occupation], but do not let this weaken your resolve."

Central to the psychological warcraft of U.S. schools is to broadcast happy images of their invasion into the lives and communities of occupied peoples. They project the false image of multicultural democracy, of benevolent compulsion. This projection is not just a cover for the work of colonization "at home," but is also one of the signal initiatives undertaken by the U.S. nation-state to promote its duplicitous image "abroad" as the guardian of innocents. Teacher preparation programs promote images of their cadettes as they descend into classrooms of captive children. They host "social justice" events for platoons of the democratic charade, co-opt the language of liberation into genocidal liberalism---and liberal companies of educators are the most dangerous as they are the front lines of the western democratic fantasy. As "Israel" lies about being the only "democracy" in the "Middle East," so too the "U.S." lies, mostly through its schools.

The lie of schooling---that it is a democratic project and a project of democracy rather than an implement of colonial control---serves as cover for devastating and depraved slaughter of peoples around the world: peoples made "uncivilized" (or, brutishly child-like) and so deserving of death of their futures. The U.S. and its hellish global gang deploy the arsenal of schooling to bolster their preeminent deceit. Schooling camouflages the only aims of colonial capitalist empires: to expand, to extract, and to exploit. Children, as futures, as links through generations, get in the way of this.

The educational branch of the war machine floods the world with images of learning and success, progress and civilization, in every occupied space possible--as if to say, "Look, we have come to rescue children, to salvage the detritus of barbaric societies, and to do so with our best and brightest." The glossy teacher preparation program pamphlet projects the image of sincere dedication, in the shape of the multicultural student teacher leaning over to engage the smiling Black child, all the while normalizing the subjection of Black peoples to suffering and premature death. All the while normalizing the need for U.S.-style democracy in the shape of bombs screaming incessantly into Gazan schools, into Gazan schoolchildren's bodies. But our resolve to truth, solidarity, and a free Palestine with living futures is unshaken.

How We Might Consider Being Called into Solidarity

Rule 3 "Never spread the occupation's propaganda, and do not contribute to instilling a sense of defeat ... Never spread panic; be supportive of the resistance."

As teachers in U.S. schools (from kindergarten through the university) designed as an aggressive propaganda arm of a fascist war state, how do we respond to the call to solidarity? How do we join the global intifada?

We observe seemingly simple responses, which align with our cardinal obligations as educators: to provoke inquiry into the truth, and to provide the skills to undertake that inquiry. Regardless of the starkly propagandistic curricula or censorship we are subjected to, we can always find ways to ask the right questions, surface the important stories, and make communities of authentic learning with students. What gets trickier is how we encounter liberal counterinsurgency.

The vast repressive liberal wing of the education machine co-opts the language of liberation, but hand-wrings over "civil discourse" and other false flags of schooling. They normalize "both side"-ism, and publicly shame our solidarity as "unprofessional." We don't panic. We don't spread their liberal genocidal propaganda, nor do we spread worry. We embrace unprofessionalism, reject that there are two sides to genocide, occupation, and colonization, refuse the cooptation of justice, and say back that they are in the tradition of genocidal movements when they leverage civility and being civilized to demarcate peoples: study tells us that killers always label people uncivilized before they normalize and necessitate their killing for democracy's sake.

Rule 4 "The enemy will broadcast images of prisoners, most likely civilians, but the goal is to suggest the rapid collapse of the resistance. Do not believe them."

As teachers joining the global intifada, we understand U.S. Black schoolchildren as prisoners. Their captive or successful faces are broadcast relentlessly to suggest the effectiveness and imperative of schooling. We do not believe the educational warmongers.

Also broadcast are the captive faces of Palestinian school children. As schools and universities---as places of refuge and learning in Gaza--are bombed with nuclear force, as schoolchildren's bodies are injured and slaughtered, as teachers are assassinated, as the U.S. occupation's congress passes curricular, aid, and other laws to suppress Palestinian schooling and learning, we see in spite of the bloodlust, a Palestinian victory. We see that Palestine has one of the highest rates of formal education in the world, especially of women and girls, and that young children forcibly starved, bombed, displaced, and orphaned, continue to say they miss school and their teachers, continue to study the Koran on bare ground, in camps.

We believe the resistance lives in the insurgent use and practice of schooling for liberation. We believe that resistance lives even in the U.S. where schooling is proto-genocidal. We believe in guerrilla teaching.

Rule 5 "The enemy will carry out tactical, qualitative operations to assassinate some symbols, and all of this is part of psychological warfare. Those who have died and those who will die will never affect the resistance's system and cohesion because the structure and formations of the resistance are not centralized but horizontal and widespread."

Liberal teacher gangs and power-driven equity-focused principals and deans in occupied U.S. universities and schools strategically attack guerrilla teachers. They mobilize joy, love, and listening as values exemplified by the school and abrogated or violated by the resistance. They form back channels to identify us as unwell, uncollegial, or unruly. As the armed resistance in Palestine operates in legitimate defense of its peoples and its futures, guerrilla educators raise consciousness, speak truth, and fight genocidal democratic education governance for global futures.

We believe we stay cohesive in the face of the many attacks by the professional pageantry by abdicating all the psychological munitions that form its power: professional organizations, conferences, professional development, foundations, boards, and many other formations that stay silent and thereby complicit in slaughter. We stand on principle and withdraw papers, refuse attendance, reject awards, decline funding, resign positions, and hold our unions accountable. We turn to what are our first duties: to study and teach. We risk collectively, so that when one of us is attacked, we are not alone.

Rule 6 "Our direct human and material losses will be much greater than the enemy's, which is natural in guerrilla wars that rely on willpower, the human element, and the extent of patience and endurance. We are far more capable of bearing the costs."

"You must understand," said Baldwin, "that in the attempt to correct so many generations of bad faith and cruelty, when it is operating not only in the classroom but in society, you will meet the most fantastic, the most brutal, and the most determined resistance. There is no point in pretending that this won't happen." When teachers and students join the global intifada, they learn that the resistance movement is blamed, and that blame is expressed in the most fantastic, most brutal violence.

What does that look like? Public holding to account of our school deans, principals, and presidents for their multiple forms of collusion in genocide is met with devastating loss. In new formations of antiblackness, identity is weaponized against the liberatory struggle, so that if the leader is Black, the members of the resistance are accused of being racist and attacking the leader, even, or especially, if the resistance is Black and Brown. They are accused of harming leaders while they and other Black and Brown leaders are simultaneously subjected to white supremacist attacks (often from Zionist organizations). Like "Israel," the leaders are rescued as victims, and the liberals, conservatives, and right wingers close ranks around this opportune heroism. Those who support the war machine are awarded, celebrated, promoted, elevated, and further empowered. Teachers who resist are sidelined, fired, demoted, disparaged, and defamed. We are isolated, alienated, and blacklisted. And this new formation is used to re-categorize Blackness, to re-designate who is a "good" or "bad" person of color.

These losses are predictable and temporary in the life of liberation struggle. But they are not insignificant, and they make way for and enshrine other losses: teachers receive death threats, are doxed, added to dangerous websites, and so on. We have to not only face and bear the losses inside schools, but recognize their links to material danger and support our colleagues and students who are targets.

Losses are countered by gains: the sacred educational duty we uphold and its spiritual award, the new alliances we form and join, the freedom of mind and purity of purpose we refine, and the inevitable victory of all occupied peoples. As teachers, if we must live, we must always utilize study to build the will to do the impossible and win, no matter how small our numbers, no matter how great the losses. And because we are in the global intifada, because the collective will spreads among millions, we can bear the losses. We must bear them as our responsibility is by nature to futures. To children, now and when they are elders, and to elders who were once children and who are always a people's child.

We can bear the loss because we recognize genocide in Gaza just as we recognize many genocides in the U.S. We accept our responsibility to fight against colonial schools as part of the resistance. As James Baldwin said to that group of teachers over six decades ago, "No American has the right to allow the present government to say, when Negro children are being bombed and hosed and shot and beaten all over the Deep South, that there is nothing we can do about it." While our primary affiliation is not "American," we understand that as people who care for and shepherd futures, we must never cower to rulers and regimes, whether of nation-states or of schools. We must always know if we are children of empire or children of liberation. There are no caveats, because Black freedom and Palestinian freedom require futures and worlds that cannot accommodate a fractionalized, partial genocide. Genocide must become an impossibility. We teach and study unfalteringly toward a world in which the concept will be impossible to make sense of.

How to Reflect on Possibility and Purpose as We Teach with the Movements for the Self-determined Liberation of Peoples Everywhere

> *Rule 7 "Today's wars are no longer just wars and clashes between armies but rather are struggles between societies."*

In what we believe are the late, barbarous stages of empire, we work inside its war machine, working toward its absolute end, teaching and studying to prefigure futures. That means we work toward futures, and with the embodiment and practice of youth: learning. We know we are in a war, that we are guerrilla teachers, learning from the resistance as we go. We know this is a battle between societies: genocidal ones and liberated ones. And we know that just because we are inside the societal organization of the school does not mean the ideological, material boundaries of the school delimit the possibilities of our solidarity. The clash is between the war machine's imperialist institutions and teachers in the global intifada moving to build an un-walled world of liberated knowledge.

> *Rule 8 "Every Palestinian (in the broad sense, meaning anyone who sees Palestine as a part of their struggle, regardless of their secondary identities), every Palestinian is on the front lines of the battle for Palestine, so be careful not to fail in your duty."*

In one of his many prescient moments, Baldwin laid out the charge to teachers: "The obligation of anyone who thinks of himself as responsible is to examine society and try to change it and to fight it — at no matter what risk. This is the only hope society has." If we adopt al-Araj's precept that we are all Palestinian, then we become Palestinian teachers, and we are responsible to futures no matter the risk. We may struggle, err, and at times fall short, but we understand we cannot fail to endeavor at every turn, in every moment, to teach and study on the front lines of the global intifada.

To stay faithful to our duty means to support and work alongside our students and all the world's students. Students are under attack. If we are on the front lines, we are required to dedicate ourselves to our students' learning and activism, and to take the risks and the hits that make space for their liberation struggle--a struggle for the future.

Notes

1. "A Talk to Teachers," James Baldwin. Delivered October 16, 1963, as "The Negro Child – His Self-Image"; originally published in *The Saturday Review*, December 21, 1963, reprinted in *The Price of the Ticket, Collected Non-Fiction 1948-1985*, St. Martins, 1985.

2. "If I Must Die," by Refaat Alareer and "If We Must Die," by Claude McKay.

3. https://www.instagram.com/p/C4TK_Pzx3Aj/?img_index=8

4. Israeli Occupation Forces.

5. Vaught, et al., *The School-Prison Trust*. University of Minnesota Press, 2022.

Gaza's Children's Lives Matter:
A Prophetic and Theological Treatise
Rev. Dr. Marshall Elijah Hatch, Sr.

War is the mechanized extinguishing of human lives. It is a grotesque enterprise. Humans justify war by claiming a moral cause, a cause or principle deemed of greater value or higher virtue than the sacredness of human life itself. A moral cause, one that is a cause good and right, is arguably limited to self-defense, or defending the defenseless, or the fight for the freedom of a people from conquest and oppression and disinheritance. The moral use of war limits trained designated combatants as mutual targets of mechanized killing. And even then, to make intentional extinguishment of human life more morally palatable, the opposing army's combatants must be equally able to self-defend and prosecute counter combat. And further, to prepare combatants for the trauma of participating in organized, mechanized killing, enemy combatants are trained to group dehumanized opposing combatants into "japs," or "krauts," or "gooks," or "chinks," or "sand niggers" "terrorists," or other others in order to create categories of disposable humanity.

Yet even philosophically just wars morally prohibit the systematic killing and harming of noncombatants. The taking of innocent civilian lives must be avoided at all costs. And in the highest ethical order, there could never be a moral justification for the collateral killing of children in war. It would constitute unforgivable sin and an existential threat to the human race. To kill children militarily, systematically, indiscriminately, and collaterally as a part of warfare is a ghastly and abominable sin against divinity and humanity. Children constitute the sacrosanct prototype of absolute innocence.

What prompts this writing? In 2024, Israel Defense Forces are prosecuting war in Gaza in reaction to the horrific October 7 Hamas attack that killed approximately 1,200 citizens in one day. Over 300 hostages were taken. Terrorism against civilians in all its forms is morally repugnant and universally considered to be unjustifiable. In spite of charges of ongoing illegal occupation, apartheid, and settler colonialism against the Israeli government, at that point Israel had moral high ground around the world. In one hundred plus days since that attack, Israeli army operations have killed over 30,000 people in Gaza, of which over 60% are women and children. It is problematic that more innocent Palestinian civilians are being killed than Palestinian combatants. We can quantify the obscene number of children being killed in Israel's military campaign, but we cannot yet calculate the number of children in Gaza who will die of disease and manufactured famine. And further, surviving children will suffer severe debilitating post-war traumas. Sowing this wind, Israelis of the future can expect to reap the whirlwind of neighborly proximity to multiple generations of orphaned, dispossessed, traumatized, vengeful Palestinian humanity.

Today, Gaza is the least safe place on earth to be a child. Three of the strongest militaries in human history, the armies of Israel, the United States, and the United Kingdom, are responsible for weaponizing the mechanized killing of tens of thousands of the most vulnerable children on earth. Divine retribution for this dastardly irony is certain to be devastatingly exacting. Gaza's children's lives do matter to God. Their lives matter with the same revelation and intensity of the Black Lives Matter movement post George Floyd. The Black Lives Matter movement of the 21st century is a philosophical and Black theological offspring of the moral and spiritual profundity of Jesus of Nazareth and his solidarity with humanity's disinherited. It is the revelation that Divinity always views the world from the bottom of empire. That is the lens that made the matter of Black lives in our context a moral imperative. The videotaped murder of George Floyd at the hands of a sworn peace officer of the state spurred a moral demand that resulted in the global Black Lives Matter movement. Morality demanded that Black lives that had mattered least under four hundred years of state-sanctioned white supremacy must now matter the most. Universal salvation is always tied to highly valuing the most vulnerable. When the human lives that mattered least are valued the most, then as a practical result all human lives will matter and no life will be devalued.

The logic of Black Lives Matter is that the most vulnerable must garner the preferred attention and protection. The spiritual and moral imperative of scripture testifies that "the last must become first." The people thought least in the power dynamics of human society are always deemed most precious in the sight of God. The wise mind of the Holy One dictates that when the interest of those in the margins of human society are brought to the center of public policy, the Kingdom of God arrives on the earth and, as in the idyllic genesis of humanity, everyone and everything flourishes. Social justice is the prerequisite for human flourishing. Without the virtue of centralizing the marginalized we will remain conflicted in constant strife. There will be "war and rumor of war." We must create a world that highly values the most vulnerable or we will all perish. Where there is no justice, there can be no peace.

This is such a time for the prophetic word and the call to spiritual awakening. Gaza with tens of thousands of children killed in the Israel-Hamas war of unequal combatants has become the moral-immoral epicenter of the planet. We are all witnesses of the first undeniable televised genocide of the 21st century. The bodies of Gaza's child martyrs are Exhibit A. The most powerful and progressive nations of the world have not found the will to stop the slaughter of children in Gaza's open- air tomb of doom. Our international institutions have been dysfunctional and, subsequently, international order is destabilized. The strong prey upon the weak with impunity. A world disorder driven by greed and cunning and amoral artificial intelligence lurks on the horizon. And the horizon is a cliff. We are entering a moral dark age of unfathomable human suffering. We peer into wars in Ukraine and Sudan and around the world and see the reflection of the future abyss. Gaza has become the ultimate test of the health of our global collective conscience. If we collectively ignore the call to address and intervene in the morally repugnant wholesale killing of children in the conduct of hyper-tech warfare upon a defenseless enclave, we may not survive as a planet and a species.

We are witnessing in real time the use of the most sophisticated technologies of warfare and propaganda and communication blackout to perfect the disinheritance of a people with child-centered genocide. The cynics call the Gaza operation "mowing the lawn." The perpetrators, the enablers, and the silent are all complicit. The world is on trial before a moral universe. The lives of Gaza's children must matter for our collective salvation. What we do or don't do for starving children bombed and trapped in the most densely populated narrow strip of real estate on earth will tell us all we need to know about the future of the human race. Until Gaza's children are protected with massive restitutions to rectify our tragic complicities in the criminal enterprise of Israeli Prime Minister Benjamin Netanyahu and his extreme right-wing cabinet, a moral and actual doomsday may be our collective destiny.

We must remind ourselves of the simple truths that peacemakers are God's children. Peace on earth is not a given but is diligently pursued by justice-seeking, peace-loving people. The "war" in Gaza has become an assault against on our common humanity. We are all called to ensure that the guilty are brought to international justice and see that the victims are repaired. Hostages and political prisoners on all sides, some of whom are children, must be freed. Either a just two-state solution or an integrated one state with equal rights for all must be decided upon. If a holy land of sacred sites and sacred texts that spawned global faith traditions and connects the three continents of humanity's original diaspora cannot find the righteous path to peace and prosperity and security, there will be little hope for the world. If we can muster up the moral courage to act definitively in saving the children of Gaza, it means that we may have it in us to figure out how to save ourselves.

And Palestine, Its People and Their Children Will Prevail: Praising and Supporting Their Radical Refusal to Be Defeated

Dr. Maulana Karenga

It is a central and grounding teaching of our sacred text, the *Husia*, that we are morally obligated to bear witness to truth and set the scales of justice in their proper place, especially among and for the voiceless, the devalued, the degraded, the poor, the vulnerable and oppressed. This sacred teaching also refers to and raises up for special concern and consideration the infant and the child, the orphan, elderly and infirm, the different and the stranger and other categories of the vulnerable, those most susceptible to harm and mistreatment. As Dr. Martin Luther King, Jr. (Washington,1986: 234) would reaffirm thousands of years later in the midst of another unjust and savage war, the war against the Vietnamese people, "We are called to speak for the weak, for the voiceless, for the victims of our nation and for those it calls 'enemy', for no document from human hands can make these humans any less our brothers (and sisters)." Indeed, honoring this ancient and ongoing African ethical imperative, we must seek and speak truth, do and demand justice in the interest of African and human good and the well-being of the world and all in it.

Indeed, we as African peoples are linked to this struggle in this time of turning in various ways as allies in struggle and as midwives and co-makers of a new unfolding history, not only for Palestine and the Palestinian people, but also for us and, indeed, for the world. For the issues raised and struggled over are issues critical to expanding the realm of freedom and justice in the world and creating just and free societies and the good and sustainable world we all want, struggle for and deserve. And as the UN and UNICEF have stated, this is a "war against children," Palestinian children. It is with this recognition and condemnation of Israel's total war practices which victimizes children most that the UN placed Israel on the list of shame, a list of nations most abusive of children in conflicts (UN, 2024).

Since the October 7, 2023 attack by the Qassem Brigade, the military wing of Hamas, on Israeli soldiers and civilians and its taking of hostages, Israel has declared and waged a total war on the Palestinian people of Gaza, bombing relentlessly and mercilessly without discriminating between civilian and soldier, killing at this writing, not counting those under the rubble, over 37,000 Palestinians, mostly children and women, wounding over 85,000 and reducing to rubble and ruin structures, objects and sites of every kind. It is a high-tech total war, testing and using AI and algorithms of death and destruction other oppressors and genocidists could only dream of, and with a worldwide support for its genocide from the US and other White-dominated countries, revealing a selective morality dishonest and deceptive in its contentions, dismissive of concepts of international law and justice and devastating to the vulnerable victims whose genocide they seek to justify.

This is being done under Israel's savage concept of self-defense as a right, not only to practice its early man morality of an eye-for-an-eye, but also to openly declare a war of vengeance, of indiscriminate and disproportionate "maximum damage," of "mowing the lawn" (the Palestinian people), of cutting off access to food, water, fuel, medical equipment and to destroy other and all the conditions necessary for life, in a word, wage war without restraint or restrictions internal or external, total war and genocide. Moving from this immoral and illegal practice of war under the guise of self-defense as whatever they want to do, they attempt to both deny genocide and justify their genocidal action by focusing exclusively on October 7 and the attack by Hamas' Qassem Brigade.

This is to act as if Israel's 76 years of mass killing, dispossessions, massive political imprisonment, sieges, destruction of villages, homes, and the infrastructure and economy of Palestine, the apartheid and occupation are all to be discounted, dismissed and forgotten (Said, 1992; Ashrawi, 1995; Abunimah, 2014; Khalidi, 2021). Instead, we are to believe and embrace their hatred of Hamas as a resistance movement and thus as a threat is the basis of their savaging the Palestinian people as a whole since 1948. And yet, in spite of the propagandistic pretense of just targeting Hamas fighters, they have not disabled or destroyed Hamas in eight months of mass murder of innocent civilians and aid workers, and saturation and indiscriminate bombing and shelling of homes, hospitals and entire residential areas; schools and universities, mosques, churches, bakeries and buildings of all kinds; museums and marketplaces; water and power systems including solar panels; agriculture and industry; rescue equipment; refugee camps and roads and routes of escape from the carnage; ambulances and other emergency vehicles; UN service and sanctuary sites, leaving no person or place safe, sound and untouched, especially children.

Some people might feel or fake confusion or be conflicted about rightly calling Israel's total war against the Palestinian people genocide for racial, religious and political reasons, or question or deny the equally overwhelming evidence of its practice of apartheid which is also a crime against humanity. And others might argue against the International Court of Justice's ruling of a "plausible case of genocide," in South Africa's case of genocide brought against Israel and hope they can pressure the Court to dismiss in its eventual final ruling the abundant and cogent evidence submitted to it. But regardless of the expected machinations, mystification and lying as a way of life, the people of Palestine know; the children, the women and the men, the victims and survivors know; and will not go quietly and meekly to their AI-determined and Amalek-defined deaths. Also, all those who have risen up across the world in resistance to this genocide and against its perpetrators and their crime partners know. For they reject the hasbara and Hitlerian lies that, as Haji Malcolm (1965: 93) taught "the science of image making," which turns the criminal into the victim and the victim into the criminal. And they will not betray the Palestinian people or their own best moral values by active or inactive complicity and cooperation in oppression.

And we, Africans, continental and diasporan, know this full well too and join in rightful resistance also. Indeed, we come from a people who have, ourselves, suffered and survived one of the greatest genocides in human history, the Holocaust of enslavement, the *Maangamizi*, a morally monstrous act of genocide that is not only against the targeted people, us, African people, but also a crime against humanity as a whole. So, we don't need to be tutored or told in simple terms the monstrous meaning and awesome evil of genocide. Also, we come from a people who have experienced and endured the savagery of segregation, US apartheid, a crime against humanity. So, we don't need to have a refresher course to recognize apartheid when we see it. And we come from a people who know what it is to be terrorized, targeted and killed, at every site: on lonely roads and busy streets, in fields, forests and swamps, in our homes, schools and universities, churches, mosques and temples, in parks and playgrounds, workplaces, cars and convenience stores. And we know the hateful face and lethal force of terrorism by an oppressive government and state-sanctioned racist vigilantes. So, we need no instruction, advice or additional information on the pernicious pathology of racist and religious hatred and hostility and the will of the ruling race and class, all turned into public policy and socially sanctioned practice. For it is both a lived and living experience, a past and present reality, and the focus of our continuing resistance.

We speak here then in defense and support of the Palestinian people vulnerable to a ruthless invading and occupying army and its supportive population, and made voiceless by the corporate media, punitive academies and limit-imposing liberals and progressives trying to suppress truth, especially on Palestine while claiming to teach and welcome it (Hill and Plitnick, 2022). They are those "who compromised the music of truth, the poetry of deep thought" (Madhubuti, 2009: 15). And they are made vulnerable and victimized by the US and European governments and cooperating citizens of the White West, especially the right-wing White evangelicals, who are active and complicit in a morally monstrous genocide of the Palestinian people with no sanctuary for anyone, children, women or men, the infant or the elder, the ill, disabled, the well, the civilian.

We especially mourn and are moved to action by the wanton bombing, sniping, shelling, starving, crushing and slaughtering of the children, which is emotionally normal and morally imperative. But we must be similarly sensitive also to the suffering and slaughtering of the people as a whole, for their suffering and slaughter are a shared atrocity and evil imposed and carried out by their oppressor and genocidist. Thus, to talk of and demonstrate serious concern for the children of Palestine and anywhere else in the world, we must have a similar moral, emotional and active concern for their families and community, for their nation. For it is in family and community that children are brought into being, nurtured, educated, affirmed, protected, provided for and guided into adulthood. Thus, the genocidal war is being waged against not only the children, but also, the source and center of the lives and future of the Palestinian children, their parents and people. They are inseparable.

Already, the killing of whole families and multiple generations has altered the lives of the children and adults in devastating psychological, physical, medical and material ways. There is a new generation of orphans, amputees, sight and hearing impaired, terrorized and traumatized children created by Israel's genocide in just eight months and similarly affected adults who have not experienced a day or space without indiscriminate and murderous bombing for eight months. Also, the forced collective starving of the people means not only the murder of the children, but also the murder of the mother and father and other family members who would have normally provided food and other life necessities for them.

There is a special evil attached to the killing of children even in peace, but especially in war. For they are wounded and killed in great numbers and in terrible and horrific ways, and they have done nothing and can do nothing worthy of this wounding and death in any way. In this Israeli genocidal war in Gaza and Palestine as a whole, the children along with others are innocent victims in a war they did not declare, provoke, contribute weapons to or provide soldiers for. And Israel, the US, and other states who are complicit and cooperative in this massive infanticide within the genocide must not and will not escape accountability and the judgment and condemnation of history and humanity.

Nor can these perpetrators escape the charge of *intentionally* killing the children and innocent civilians. For the use of 2,000 lb. and even smaller bombs dropped intentionally and continuously in crowded spaces in a country where half the people are children indicates a willingness and intention to kill them. Nor can the Israeli Occupation Forces (IOF) claim these indiscriminate bombings as mistakes or camouflage the massacres using morally questionable concepts of *collateral* damage and *acceptable murders* carried out against innocent children and unarmed civilians to kill selected targets deemed of high value to the killers. This, in any seriously moral sense, demonstrates a repulsively depraved disregard for human life and human rights, life being the first and most fundamental human right with freedom being an essential and indispensable correlative right as Haji Malcolm taught (Lomax, 1963: 150). And it is important to note here that the problem is not simply Netanyahu, the IOF, the right-wing extremists, and the settlers, but also the Israeli public who have registered in poll after poll an overwhelming majority's commitment to this genocidal campaign. And the few who dare to speak out and resist are suppressed, ostracized and punished.

To kill without conscious and human consideration, the oppressor, especially the colonizer and settler, attempts to demonize and dehumanize the oppressed. As Frantz Fanon (1968: 41, 42) notes, "It is not enough for the settler to delimit physically" and to kill mercilessly. But "as if to show the totalitarian character of colonial exploitation, the settler paints the native as a sort of quintessence of evil." The White settler poses his alleged purity and humanity against the alleged impurity and animality of the native. "In fact, the terms the settler uses when he mentions the native, are zoological terms," i.e., "reptilian motions," "breeding swarms," etc. Thus, government officials called the Palestinians "beasts" and "a beastly people" and twistedly argued and acted out the morally depraved contention that all, including children, are worthy of the most horrible deaths. For as the President of Israel stated, "It is an entire nation out there that is responsible." And other governmental officials have said all Palestinians in Gaza are the enemy, including "its elderly and its women, its cities and its villages, its properties and its infrastructure."

But as Aimé Césaire (1972: 20) tells us, the oppressor, the genocidist, "the colonizer, who in order to ease his conscience gets into the habit of seeing the other man as an *animal,* accustoms himself to treating him like an animal, and tends objectively to transform *himself* into an animal." And, as we can see today, it is through this self-transformation, this self-animalization, they are able and eager to kill children, women and men without conscience, starve them to death, force them to die of thirst, kill their teachers and professors, doctors, journalists, intellectuals and professionals and destroy their homes, hospitals, schools, libraries, universities, their farms, fields and fruit trees, and other food sources, their archives, museums and heritage sites, and pollute their air, water and land, and thus commit physical genocide, cultural genocide, domicide and ecocide without conscience or constraint, and without the demonstrated capacity for human empathy for the Palestinians and to admit the radical evil of their genocidal sentiments, thoughts and practices.

Thus, Israel offers a self-serving and convenient hasbara propaganda claim that it is engaging in mass killing of the children, and the ill, elderly and innocent civilians because the resistance movement, Hamas, hides among the people and uses them as human shields, a claim the fascists made earlier to bomb Ethiopian hospitals and other protected sites. This spurious claim of human shielding hides the fact that all resistance movements are embedded among the people. For it is there that they live, work, serve and come forth to resist the invader and the oppressor. This is clear, not only in all revolutionary movements in history, but also in the history of the French resistance and other European resistance movements against Nazi conquests and domination, including Jewish resistance.

These resistance movements did not meet in the public square or on a hill and call for the invader and genocidists to come and get them, but fought the enemy where they were attacked in their own space, a space they have a right to live in with their families and communities in dignity, peace, security and freedom. And they have a right to resist domination, deprivation and degradation imposed on them. Indeed, it is the enemy oppressor and genocidist that disguise themselves and hide among the people to sabotage, subvert and kill them and rescue their comrades or hostages and, in the process, commit vicious atrocities and slaughter in the midst of the people, killing hundreds. And this they did in Gaza to recover four by slaughter even though previous negotiations had led to the release of over a hundred.

Also, it's important to note that it is Israel, itself, which has historically and continuously used children and adults as human shields as reported by human rights organizations such as Human Rights Watch, Amnesty International, and B'Tselem, as well as the recent UN Report listing Israel among the rogue states that abuse children in war and occupation. Documented reports affirm that they have tied Palestinian children to vehicles, forced them to walk in front of them in the line of fire, used them to test booby traps and remove objects suspected of being explosives, and coerced them to provide information on or lure people they suspect and target to capture or kill.

As we contemplate this unfolding reordering of the world, let us pay rightful recognition and praise to the Palestinian people for their incredible resilience, their radical refusal to be defeated and their righteous resistance in every way possible, eventually exposing the systemic savagery of the occupation, siege and genocide by Israel and its crime partners, and winning new allies in resistance. Let us also recognize and praise the consistent reciprocal support of Palestine liberation and audacious legal and political initiatives of South Africa, defying all threats to charge Israel with genocide at the International Court of Justice (ICJ), win a decision of "plausible" commission of genocide and return to achieve another ruling to order Israel to stop its genocidal attack against Gaza in Rafah, Palestine. We are at a pivotal period in human history signified in meaningful ways by struggles around ending Israel's genocidal war and occupation in Palestine which involve issues of the right to life, freedom, justice, security of persons and peoples, and the right to all the material and other conditions and capacities essential to life.

This world-encompassing struggle has a reach and relevance of great importance. First of all, it reaffirms the Palestinian people's radical refusal to be defeated and their and our faith that they will eventually prevail and reclaim their freedom and rebuild their lives. Moreover, it has built a valuable unity across borders in transformative struggle, educating the world to another more truthful narrative than that of the oppressors, and confronting this interrelated world order of White supremacy and its unrepentantly predatory relatives: racism, racial capitalism, settler colonialism, imperialism and apartheid on campus, in community and on the world stage of history (Asante, 2003; Karenga, 2017).

Also, an important achievement of this world-encompassing struggle is the breaching of the white wall of immunity from criticism and impunity from accountability of the state of Israel. And it exposes Israel's falsified image of victimizer as victim, aggressor as the aggrieved, and the object of a contrived existential threat while being an aggressor and occupying nation and an actual and proven threat to the existence of the Palestinian people in real time and in radically evil genocidal ways.

Thus, we link struggles for a new world and support the Palestinian people's liberation struggle to free themselves, to build their own country and state, to live in peace with all their neighbors, and to forge a secure, good and meaningful life and future for their children. And we reaffirm our commitment to that new world for all the people of the world, working and striving for a freedom not yet regained, a justice not yet achieved and a sure-to-come ever expansive life not yet lived and shared for all the liberated and free peoples of the world.

References

Abunimah, Ali. *The Battle for Justice in Palestine.* Haymarket, 2014.

Asante, Molefi. *Erasing Racism: The Survival of the American Nation.* Prometheus Books, 2003.

Ashrawi, Hanan. *This Side of Peace.* Simon and Schuster, 1995.

Césaire, Aimé. *Discourse on Colonialism.* Monthly Review Press, 1972.

Fanon, Frantz. *Wretched of the Earth.* Grove, 1968.

Khalidi, Rashid. *The Hundred Years' War on Palestine.* Metropolitan, 2021.

Karenga, Maulana. "Revisiting Race and Racism: A Critical Examination of a Pathology of Oppression," in *Race in America: How a Pseudoscientific Concept Shaped Human Interaction,* Volume 1, Patricia Reid-Merritt (ed.), pp. 23-42., Santa Barbara, Praeger, 2017.

Karenga, Maulana (Ed.). *Selections From the Husia: Sacred Wisdom of Ancient Egypt.* University of Sankore Press, 1984.

Hill, Marc Lamont, and Mitchell Plitnick. *Except for Palestine: The Limits of Progressive Politics.* The New Press, 2022.

Lomax, Louis. *When the Word Is Given. The World Publishing Company,* 1963.

Malcolm X. *Malcolm X Speaks.* Grove, 1965.

Madhubuti, Haki. *Liberation Narratives: New and Collected Poems 1966-2009.* Chicago, Third World Press, 2009.

Said, Edward. *The Question of Palestine.* Vintage, 1992.

United Nations. Children and Armed Conflict, Report of the Secretary-General, https://documents.un.org/doc/undoc/gen/n24/095/07/ pdf/n2409507.pdf?token=hya1nUjCb7H67UWHZD&fe=true, retrieved June 18, 2024.

Washington, James Melvin. (1986). *A Testament of Hope: The Essential Writings of Martin Luther King Jr.* Harper and Row, 1986.

A Prayer for the Children of Gaza

Rahiel Tesfamariam

Dear God,

We come before You with immense humility and endless grief, as these horrific, genocidal times remind us of our human limitations. We yearn for You to free us from our sense of powerlessness. We lay our prayers down before You, trusting You to restore wholeness to people and places that evil forces have sought to destroy. We know that You are more powerful than all these systems and governments that have failed us.

You loved us enough to give up Your divinity and become one with our suffering. You loved us enough to promise Your children resurrection from the tombs of this world. Through Your story, we know that pain can be alchemized into power. We put our faith in You and You alone. Please equip us with the tenacity needed to ensure "[we] have fought the good fight, [we] have finished the race, [we] have kept the faith (2 Timothy 4:7, ESV).

God, our hearts have been broken daily for months now, watching the most vulnerable of society buried under the rubble. We have seen and heard the agonizing cries of Your children. Their burns. Their bones. Their empty bellies. How many times did they beg for mercy? How many times did they cry out for their mothers and fathers? How many times did they ask for an end to the living hell — with no end in sight?

Today, our prayers are for all the children of Gaza — the living and the dead. May the spirits of the survivors not be crushed by the world's failure to protect them. May Your babies arrive at their final destination of eternal Paradise and be met by You and a chorus of heavenly angels.

God, please remind the children of Gaza that You knew them before You formed them in their mother's womb (Jeremiah 1:5) and "even the very hairs of [their] head are all numbered" (Luke 12:7, KJV). Their fingerprints were drawn by You. You know their innermost thoughts. Fortify their infant minds and hearts. Build a hedge of protection around their spirits so that that they will never lose their childlike faith and innocence. As we become increasingly small in their eyes, may You become larger than life. Larger than tanks. Larger than hate. Larger than empire. Larger than apartheid regimes and settler colonialists. Nurse the children of Gaza back to wholeness and serenity. Bless them to see the day when a free Palestine will be born.

We pray that the children of Gaza would cling so tightly to Your peace that the bombs are silenced forever. We pray that they would hide themselves so deep in Your love that they would become unreachable to the oppressor. Hold them so tight in Your arms that they smell Your sweet, eternal fragrance and not the toxic air all around them. May Your presence grant protection, safety, sustenance, comfort, unconditional love, and unspeakable joy. Cleanse their eyes of all that they have witnessed. Wipe out the haunting images of execution and collective punishment. Plant in them the seeds of healing and restoration. And for the ones who will meet death prematurely, we pray that their souls would rise above the ashes, soar beyond the warfare, and enter a realm where they become eternally untouchable. May they be reborn as spiritual warriors with an insatiable appetite for liberation, love, peace, and justice.

We pray that the children of Gaza not only survive but would resurrect — in this life and the next. Resurrect from hopelessness and despair. May they triumphantly stand on top of the rubble and fiercely tell the world their stories of resilience, resistance, and redemption. May their audacity create a new generation of freedom fighters. May we all become disciples of liberation willing to go to the ends of the earth for them and future generations. God, please empower us to build a better world for the survivors. Help us draw up a blueprint for a new world order in honor of the martyrs. One greater than anything that our minds can presently hope for or imagine.

We pray for an immediate, permanent ceasefire. May the injured get life- saving help, the masses be fed and nourished, families be reunited, and orphans get connected to loving guardians. May the displaced have the right of return and the resources needed to rebuild their homes. May the schools, hospitals, mosques, and institutions be restored and flourish from then on. May Gaza be fully healed and reclaimed by its people. May the blockade end with Gazans and all Palestinians having freedom of movement. May no oppressive government in the world have the power to control the food and water supply of people they seek to subjugate. We pray that You would hold every State leader who has been complicit in this genocide accountable in the spiritual realm. We pray that the people of occupied Palestine would have the right to self-determination. We pray for a new generation of journalists and filmmakers who will document how a free Palestine was established and sustained.

God, please ensure that the children of Gaza never cease dreaming, imagining, and believing that You have "plans for peace *and* well-being and not for disaster, to give [them] a future and a hope" (Jeremiah 29:11,

Amplified). Bless them to experience Glory — one rooted in permanent, never-ending liberation from all forms of oppression. We thank You for being a God who will not allow sacrificial lambs to be slaughtered without all of humanity bowing down in repentance and experiencing everlasting transformation. We declare victory in the name of all that is good and righteous in this world and the next.

In Your Holy and Matchless Name We Pray,

Addendum I

1948: ISRAEL, SOUTH AFRICA, AND THE QUESTION OF GENOCIDE*
Robin D. G. Kelley

The UN's failure to dismantle the colonial order foreclosed the application of the Genocide Convention to Israel, South Africa, and the United States.

If the United Nations decides to amputate a part of Palestine in order to establish a Jewish state, no force on earth could prevent blood from flowing there. ... [O]nce such bloodshed has commenced, no force on earth can confine it to the borders of Palestine itself.

— Dr. Mohamed Hussein Heykal Pasha, Egyptian delegate to UN Ad Hoc Committee on Palestine, 1947

South Africa's application to the International Court of Justice (ICJ) instituting proceedings against Israel for violating the UN Genocide Convention sent U.S. officials into a frenzy. More than 200 members of Congress signed a bipartisan letter condemning the charges as "grossly unfounded and defamatory." On Feb. 6, 2024, Representatives John James, a Black Republican from Michigan, and Florida Democrat Jared Moskowitz introduced a bill meant to punish South Africa. The bill falsely asserts that the governing African National Congress (ANC) supports Hamas and accuses ANC leaders of antisemitism for "expressing concern of 'escalating violence'" and describing the war on civilians in Gaza as "genocide." The bill makes no mention of the more than 30,000 Palestinians killed and at least 72,000 wounded in Gaza in the course of more than 160 days, the roughly 1.9 million displaced people, and at least 399 Palestinians killed by settlers and Israeli occupation forces in the West Bank and East Jerusalem since Oct. 7. The Biden administration must know that the ICJ's finding of a plausible risk of genocide implicates the U.S. as a party to Israel's crimes. But rather than withhold its financial and military resources and do what is required of UN member states — act decisively to stop the genocide — the Senate voted to send Israel a whopping $14 billion to finish the job, more than triple the aid the U.S. typically sends Israel every year. Bipartisan fealty to Israel, no matter the consequences, is unsurprising. The apoplectic tone of the attacks on the case has much to do with who filed the complaint with the ICJ, however.

The ANC and its allies that make up the tripartite alliance (the

Communist Party and the Congress of South African Trade Unions) have for decades been declared enemies of both the U.S. and Israel. Before the end of formal apartheid in 1994, South Africa, Israel, and the U.S. formed a very different tripartite alliance committed to the defense of racial capitalism, apartheid, and Zionism. The U.S. and South Africa in particular have maintained strong economic ties since the early 20th century. By 1948, South Africa's mining and manufacturing sectors had absorbed considerable flows of American capital. As white "republics" built on the exploitation and disenfranchisement of Black labor, they shared a mutual defense of racial segregation and a zealous opposition to communism. Anticommunism, especially during the Cold War, provided ideological cover for the suppression of all opposition movements. Just as the U.S. promoted Israel as "the only democracy in the Middle East," it regarded South Africa as its closest ally on the African continent. All three nations allied to suppress communism and "terrorism" — namely, the forces fighting for the liberation of Palestine, against apartheid, and for revolutionary change in the U.S. — through joint counterinsurgency, shared intelligence, arms sales, and mutual military buildup.

The insurgents built their own ties with one another. Black solidarity between the U.S. and South Africa predates World War I, and their respective connections to the Palestinian liberation movement can be traced to the early 1960s. Their ties deepened in the 1970s, when the UN General Assembly approved the Convention on the Suppression and Punishment of the Crime of Apartheid, passed a resolution declaring that "zionism is a form of racism and racial discrimination," recognized the Palestine Liberation Organization (PLO) and the ANC, and sought to expel Israel and South Africa from its body. (They managed to suspend South Africa in 1974, which lasted until the ANC came to power 20 years later.) Israel's occupation of Gaza, the West Bank, and East Jerusalem following the 1967 war came to resemble the colonial violence in southern Africa, especially as the PLO, the Popular Front for the Liberation of Palestine (PFLP), and other armed groups escalated their resistance. The PLO and the ANC maintained strong ties, and decades after the downfall of apartheid, the ANC's solidarity with Palestine has not wavered. The ANC has consistently supported the BDS campaign since 2012.

It might feel like a moment of poetic justice to watch the victims of the old tripartite alliance lead efforts to protect Palestinians. But one wonders, given Israel's documented history of ethnic cleansing and a 17-year siege that has turned Gaza into a massive concentration camp, why it has taken so long for any country to ask the ICJ to investigate Israel for violating the Genocide Convention. Article II of the convention defines the term to mean any effort to "destroy, in whole or in part, a national, ethnical, racial or religious group" by causing "serious bodily or mental harm" to group members, imposing "conditions of life calculated to bring about its physical destruction in whole or in part," which includes preventing births. I am not interested in debating whether Israel is, or has ever been, guilty of genocide. I believe the evidence for genocide dating back to the 1948 Nakba (catastrophe) is irrefutable. Instead, I contend that the UN's failure to dismantle the colonial order, buttressed by Cold War imperatives, foreclosed the application of international law, particularly the Genocide Convention, to Israel, South Africa, and the United States. While the U.S. has occasionally used its veto power in the Security Council to shield both Israel and South Africa from accountability to international law, during the first decade of the UN's existence it rarely had to. Israel not only had the votes in the General Assembly but also, similar to South Africa, never had to face charges of genocide. More than two decades would pass before the General Assembly treated both countries as pariah states. Perhaps because the Holocaust became the paradigmatic case of genocide, the threshold of proof was very high — arguably too high. The convention turned into a tool of last resort, rendering it a deeply flawed instrument to prevent genocide.

The state of Israel, the UN Declaration of Human Rights, and the Genocide Convention were all "born" in 1948, in the shadow of the Holocaust and in the light of the recently formed United Nations. This was also the year South Africa officially became an apartheid state, although the policies introduced by the largely Afrikaner National Party did not radically depart from three centuries of colonialism, mineral extraction, and exploitation of African labor. Nevertheless, apartheid seemed anachronistic in an era of African independence and civil rights. Israel and South Africa were both settler-colonial regimes founded on violent dispossession that maintained some form of military rule over subject populations at a time when colonialism was said to be dying and the UN was supposed to usher in a new world order. Dr. Fayez A. Sayegh, renowned scholar and rapporteur of the special committee established under the International Convention on the Elimination of All Forms of Racial Discrimination, underscored in a 1970 essay the incongruity of Israel's settler-colonial project "in a historical era marked by universal rejection of colonialism in principle and near-total liquidation of colonial empires in practice." But despite the various charters, declarations, and conventions that confirmed human equality and condemned discrimination, the UN was founded on the principles of what the historian Mark Mazower calls "imperial internationalism." Its principal architects represented nations that still held colonies and/or practiced racial segregation. It was a South African prime minister, General Jan Smuts, who added the phrase "human rights" to the UN Charter. Unsurprisingly,

Smuts's elevated role as statesman did not sit well with the Black majority back home. The Non-European Unity Movement, a multiracial coalition with ties to the Workers Party of South Africa, issued a statement in July 1945 informing the world that South Africa's nonwhite population "live and suffer under a tyranny very little different from Nazism," and thus "it is ludicrous that this same South African Herrenvolk should speak abroad of a new beginning, of shaping a new world order, whereas in actuality all they wish is the retention of the present tyranny in South Africa, and its extension to new territories."

W. E. B. Du Bois and Mohandas Gandhi tried in vain to persuade the UN's architects to declare colonialism a crime against humanity. If this were not done, Du Bois warned: "There will be at least 750,000,000 colored and Black folk inhabiting colonies owned by white nations, who will have no rights that the white people of the world are bound to respect. Revolt on their part can be put down by military force; they will have no right of appeal to the Council or the Assembly; they will have no standing before the International Court of Justice." Du Bois's appeals went nowhere because the UN was designed to recognize nations and not peoples. Only nations had standing, which meant an attack on colonialism was an assault on the sovereignty of the colonizing nations. During its formative years, the UN distinguished "civilized nations" from the rest, a hierarchy consistent with its founding commitment to preserving the Anglo-American alliance over the freedom of 750 million people in Africa, Asia, and the Caribbean.

The UN Convention on the Prevention and Punishment of the Crime of Genocide could have been an instrument for victims of colonial violence to seek relief and justice. The convention was the brainchild of Raphael Lemkin, the distinguished Polish Jewish jurist credited with coining the term "genocide" by combining genos, the Greek word for "race" or a group of people claiming common descent, with cide, the Latin suffix for "killing." The word first appeared in print in his 1944 book, *Axis Rule in Occupied Europe*, followed by the Genocide Convention, which came before the United Nations in 1946. After two years of debate, the General Assembly approved the convention on Dec. 9, 1948, ratified by some member states in October 1950, and put it in force the next year.

Lemkin's best-known work focused on the Nazi extermination of Jews and Poles and the Armenian genocide under the Ottoman Empire, but colonialism was an important frame of reference. He considered past massacres of Indigenous peoples in the Americas and the Atlantic slave trade examples of genocide and directed students to study Belgium's atrocities in the Congo and Germany's genocide against Namibia. His definition of genocide was far more expansive than what ended up in the final draft of the convention. He deemed the destruction or erasure of culture an act of genocide, but his resistance to reducing genocidal acts to distinct categories led him to hesitate calling it "cultural genocide." Yet an early draft by the ad hoc committee did mention "cultural genocide," which it defined as "any deliberate act committed with intent to destroy the language, religion or culture of a national, racial or religious group" through banning the use of specific languages or "destroying, or preventing the use of, libraries, museums, schools, historical monuments, places of worship or other cultural institutions and objects of the group." Since acts of erasure and destruction are common features of colonialism, the inclusion of the phrase would have left more Western nations vulnerable to the charge of genocide. Little wonder the U.S., France, Canada, and the Netherlands were among the most fervent critics of the phrase.

Lemkin had some blind spots, notably underestimating the structural violence and racist subjugation required to maintain the settler state, especially within modern herrenvolk republics such as the United States and South Africa. He would come to recognize this order of structural violence as genocide by the end of his life, but not during the convention's formative years. In 1951, when William L. Patterson, a Black Communist and the executive director of the Civil Rights Congress, and Paul Robeson submitted a 240-page petition to the UN charging the United States with committing genocide against Black people, Lemkin accused the authors of being "un-American," bent on sabotaging the U.S. Senate's ratification of the convention and diverting "attention away from the crimes of genocide" perpetrated in the Soviet Union. The provocatively titled *We Charge Genocide: The Historic Petition to the United Nations for Relief From a Crime of the United States Government Against the Negro People* documented hundreds of incidents of anti-Black violence — from police killing to lynching — just in the six years since the end of the war and drew on the convention to argue that systematic violence and terrorism was state policy. In a letter to the *New York Times*, Lemkin claimed the authors confused "genocide with discrimination." Contending that the numbers of those killed or harmed were so low that the case for genocide must rest on "serious mental harm," he then poses a rhetorical question: "Can one be guilty of genocide when one frightens a Negro? Obviously not, because fear alone cannot be considered as serious mental harm as meant by the authors of the convention; the act is not directed against the Negro population of the country and by no stretch of imagination can one discover in the United States an intent or plan to exterminate the Negro population, which is increasing in conditions of evident prosperity and progress."

A vast majority of African Americans begged to differ. In fact,

Black journalists recognized the applicability of the Genocide Convention in the U.S. before the release of *We Charge Genocide*. On Oct. 21, 1950, the *New York Amsterdam News* ran an article headlined "UN Law May Be Hard on Dixie," arguing that the "lynching of Negroes in the United States [and] race destruction in the Union of South Africa" would be considered crimes of genocide. Southern senators also understood the implications immediately. Having consistently opposed a federal anti-lynching law, they believed that the convention would be used to prosecute lynchers and would not support it without assurances that it could not be used against the U.S. for treatment of its own citizens. The U.S. did not ratify the Genocide Convention until 1988. Meanwhile, Lemkin changed his mind, influenced by Ruth Benedict's *Race: Science and Politics* (1940). According to his biographer, Lemkin's unfinished manuscript *Introduction to the Study of Genocide* included "the lynching of African Americans … [as] acts of genocide in the United States legitimized by race thinking."

South Africa joined the U.S. in refusing to ratify the convention and did not become a party to the convention until 1998. The apartheid government would not agree to pass complementary domestic laws, prosecute perpetrators of genocide in domestic courts, or extradite people wanted for the crime of genocide. Its position was predictable. The 1948 election of the largely Afrikaner National Party was considered a retreat even from General Smuts's United Party — actual Nazis made up the new regime. National Party leader John Vorster declared in 1942, "We stand for Christian Nationalism which is an ally of National Socialism"; he later served as prime minister from 1966 to 1978. The deepening fascist turn should be understood as a response to heightened Black opposition during the 1940s, when African miners waged a massive national strike in 1946, and the ANC Youth League pushed its parent organization to support mass uprisings against consumer and transportation racism. The National Party promised separation of the races and the complete disfranchisement of all nonwhites. Once in power, it passed a slate of apartheid laws — what the journalist and Communist activist Brian Bunting wryly called "South Africa's Nuremberg laws." During the first three years alone, under prime minister Daniël F. Malan, the new regime expelled Indians from Parliament, curtailed Coloured voting rights, outlawed interracial marriage, excluded nearly all Africans from receiving unemployment insurance, assigned every person to a racial category defined by the state, designated race groups to specific locations, required Africans to carry passes to monitor and control their movement, and under the Suppression of Communism Act effectively outlawed every opposition movement in South Africa.

A Nazi-led apartheid government did not diminish South Africa's standing in the UN. In 1946, before the National Party came to power, India filed a complaint against South Africa for passing a law severely limiting where Asians could purchase land, arguing that it violated the UN Charter's prohibition on racial discrimination. In its defense, South Africa — with support from the U.S., the U.K., Belgium, Canada, New Zealand, and the Netherlands — invoked a separate clause in the UN Charter prohibiting member states from interfering in the affairs of another nation. India prevailed, but South Africa simply ignored the resolution and in 1948 passed even more draconian anti-Asian legislation as part of a slate of apartheid measures. In December 1950, the General Assembly passed a resolution condemning apartheid but referring only to anti-Indian discrimination. South Africa continued to enjoy the protection of the Security Council until 1960, when the council adopted a resolution deploring the police killing of 69 unarmed African protesters in the township of Sharpeville. Three years later came the first meeting of a Special Committee on the Policies of Apartheid. In 1966, the General Assembly declared apartheid a crime against humanity. The main source of tension between the apartheid regime and the UN, however, was South Africa's occupation of Namibia.

Like Israel with its occupation of Palestine, South Africa ruled Namibia as a colony in an era of decolonization. But as legal scholar Noura Erakat observes, unlike the case of Israel, the UN had recognized since at least 1946 that South Africa's occupation of what was then called South West Africa violated international law and chose to use "the legal infrastructure within the United Nations to shepherd Namibia to independence." A German colony since the 1880s, Namibia was the site of the first 20th-century genocide: Between 1904 and 1908 German settlers massacred between 40,000 and 80,000 Herero people (about 80 percent of their population) and 10,000 Nama people (about half of their population). During World War I, South Africa occupied the colony and held it as a League of Nations mandate after Germany's defeat. Instead of restoring Indigenous land rights, the South African government encouraged German and white South African settlement, forcing the Africans into the largely uninhabited territory around the Kunene River. After the collapse of the League of Nations during World War II and the creation of the UN, Namibia was supposed to become a UN Trust Territory. But South Africa refused to enter a trusteeship — the Smuts government and subsequent regimes wanted to annex Namibia outright. The Africans wanted freedom. In 1947, a delegation of Nama leaders petitioned the UN secretary-general to demand the immediate return of their lands and restoration of their sovereignty. When the UN rejected South Africa's request to annex the territory, the Parliament under Malan passed the South West Africa Amendment Act (1949), moving further toward illegal annexation by giving white settlers in Namibia representation in Parliament. The General Assembly asked for an advisory opinion from the ICJ, which issued separate opinions in 1950, 1955, and 1956, all declaring South Africa's refusal to allow Namibia to be placed under trusteeship illegal. Because the opinions were not enforceable, South Africa continued to defy international law, imposing apartheid laws and tightening repression. In 1966, the UN General Assembly passed a resolution ending the mandate and launching a new trusteeship in preparation for Namibia's independence, but South Africa refused to leave. In 1960, the newly formed South West African People's Organisation (SWAPO) launched an armed struggle for independence.

Israel signed and ratified the Genocide Convention promptly and without reservations.

Unlike that of South Africa, Israel's founding was treated by much of the world as an unmitigated triumph. Zionists believed it fulfilled the dream of a Jewish state in Palestine, authorized by God Himself in accordance with the Hebrew Bible. For survivors of the Holocaust, Israel became a safe haven for Jewish resettlement and the vehicle through which Germany could pay reparations. Labor Zionists looked to Palestine as a potential socialist promised land. In fact, the international Communist movement's support for Zionism and Israel's ruling party, the Mapai or Workers Party, obscured Israel's formation as a settler-colonial state. Moshe Dayan, a military hero in the Nakba, harbored no illusions: "Before [the Palestinians'] very eyes we are possessing the land and villages where they, and their ancestors, have lived. ... We are the generation of colonizers, and without the gun barrel we cannot plant a tree and build a home."

By 1947, the creation of some kind of Jewish state in Palestine was a *fait accompli*; the question was whether it would be one binational state or two separate states. The British planned to withdraw and transfer the responsibility for determining Palestine's future to the United Nations. A majority of Zionists wanted a state of their own and believed all the land, Eretz Israel, belonged to them. Yet they accepted UN Resolution 181, passed on Nov. 29, 1947, dividing Palestine into Jewish and Arab states. The partition plan set aside 56 percent of the land for a Jewish state and 44 percent for the Palestinians. Arab leaders were never consulted and did not agree to the plan. Palestinians argued that the partition was illegal and unjust, and asked that the matter be referred to the ICJ for an advisory opinion, but pressure from the United States blocked it.

Mapai Party leaders publicly accepted the terms of the agreement but secretly prepared to wage war to expel the Palestinians and seize additional territory. The British were on their way out, so the narrative that the war for Israel's independence was an anti-imperialist struggle begs credulity. The pretext for war was the presence of Arab armies dispatched either to protect the borders with Syria, Lebanon, Jordan, Iraq, and Egypt or ostensibly to protect Palestinian villages outside the designated boundaries of the Jewish state. But the Arab states had financial and geopolitical interests in limiting Israel's expansion that were not necessarily shared with Palestinians. Jordan's King Abdullah I, for example, wanted to annex the West Bank — which the partition plan designated as part of the Palestinian state — and made a secret agreement with the Zionists not to intervene in the war in exchange for the West Bank. Moreover, David Ben-Gurion, the Zionist leader who became Israel's first prime minister, knew the Arab armies posed no serious threat. Nevertheless, he used fear to mobilize Jewish support and sway world opinion by making public statements comparing Arabs to Nazis and warning of "a second Holocaust." In private, he used language similar to that of colonial officers preparing for a campaign. The man who in his younger days fashioned himself a "Zionist Lenin" wrote in his diary on Jan. 1, 1948: "There is a need now for strong and brutal reaction. We need to be accurate about timing, place and those we hit. If we accuse a family — we need to harm them without mercy, women and children included. Otherwise, this is not an effective reaction. During the operation there is no need to distinguish between guilty and not guilty."

Under Ben-Gurion's leadership, Israel's militias — the Haganah, Irgun, the Stern gang, the Palmach — waged a deliberate, well-organized campaign to terrorize, kill or injure, and dispossess Palestinians; raze their villages; take or destroy their property; and above all take their land. The architects of the campaign laid out a military strategy across four different plans, the most consequential and far-reaching being Plan D, or Plan Dalet. Adopted on March 10, 1948, the "plan" entailed using terrorism as a strategy of elimination. Zionist paramilitary groups were instructed to raze villages "by setting fire to them, by blowing them up, and by planting mines in their rubble," and to encircle others, conduct searches, and force people to flee; when faced with resistance, "the armed forces must be wiped out and the population expelled outside the borders of the state." From December 1947 to July 1949, Zionist militias drove three-quarters of a million people, 80 percent of the Palestinian population, from their land; destroyed or emptied over 500 villages; and demolished homes, sometimes setting them ablaze or blowing them up while families were still inside. Men were lined up and shot, women killed and raped, children shot, a pregnant woman bayoneted. Wholesale massacres in the villages of Deir Yassin and Tantura are etched in Palestinian collective memory. The cruelties are legion. In Haifa, the militias rolled barrels of explosives and large steel balls into Palestinian neighborhoods, followed by a generous stream of oil and gasoline, which they then set alight.

By the armistice of 1949, the state of Israel occupied 78 percent of Palestine. Western nations accepted Israel's new borders, but the Arab states refused to recognize the state of Israel unless it allowed Palestinian refugees to return — an impossibility, because the point of the forced population transfer was for Israel to maintain demographic dominance. The roughly 160,000 Palestinians remaining within Israel's borders were placed under military administration until 1966. Egypt, Jordan, Syria, and Lebanon reluctantly absorbed tens of thousands of Nakba survivors, though the responsibility for providing necessities like food, shelter, and education fell to the UN Relief and Works Agency (UNRWA).

The Nakba must be understood as both a crime against humanity and organized armed robbery. Israelis seized land and homes. They also stole furniture, rugs, jewelry, money, radios, and other valuable items. As the Palestinian historian Nur Masalha shows, in Jaffa (now part of Tel Aviv), Acre, Lydda, and other cities, Palestinian-owned businesses were left intact so that they could be taken over by Israeli entrepreneurs. Tens of thousands of acres of olive and fruit groves that Palestinians had owned and cultivated produced enough fruit to account for nearly 10 percent of Israel's foreign currency earnings from exports in 1951. Arabic place names were changed to Hebrew, and to ensure the erasure the Jewish National Fund (JNF) planted forests on the land of destroyed Palestinian villages. Israeli settlers seized or destroyed personal archives and appropriated a massive body of literature in Arabic, part of which ended up in Israel's National Library. Being forced to leave behind precious texts and artifacts to live in a tent or a refugee camp is what is meant by "cultural genocide." To be displaced from the land of one's family and ancestors, from the deep social bonds of the village and its churches, mosques, and schools, from ancient olive trees that have anchored Palestinian culture, is also cultural genocide.

In contrast, in 1947, the U.S. military government in West Germany passed a law for the purposes of restoring property seized from Jews under Nazi rule. In 1952, the German government agreed to pay restitution for what historian Marilyn Henry categorizes as "identifiable assets, including machinery, real estate, business enterprises, and cultural properties." Palestinians received no such compensation. Israel's Absentees' Property Law of 1950 transferred all property owned or used by Palestinian refugees to the state of Israel, and then denied their right to return or reclaim their losses. Even Palestinians living inside

Israel's 1948 borders are declared "present absentees" if they are not physically on their property and ineligible to reclaim it. Another 1950 law transferred confiscated Palestinian land and private property to Israel's Development Authority, which turned over much of it to the World Zionist Organization's Jewish Agency for Israel and the JNF to support migration to Israel and forestation on Palestinian land. A land acquisition law passed in 1953 empowered the state to confiscate Palestinian land for military use and Jewish settlements.

Just five years into Israel's history it had begun to resemble South Africa. So where was the UN Charter? The invocation of the Genocide Convention? The outrage of member states? Criticism came almost exclusively from Arab states. In October 1950, Egypt's UN ambassador, Mahmoud Bey Fawzi, complained that Israel had conducted a "large-scale military operation" to drive Bedouins from a demilitarized zone near Jericho and decried the deteriorating conditions for Palestinian refugees. "While we are pondering and debating here," he told the Security Council, "many thousands of fellow human beings in Palestine are subjected to a most inhuman treatment, expelled from their homes, and forced to seek shelter elsewhere against the cold and the hardships of a speedily approaching winter." In response, Israeli ambassador Abba S. Eban dismissed Egypt's "atrocity stories" as "unsubstantiated by any creditable source."

The atrocities continued, and the UN began to take notice. In 1956, retaliating against Egyptian President Gamal Abdel Nasser's decision to nationalize the French- and British-owned Suez Canal Company, Britain, France, and Israel invaded Egypt. Israel took advantage of the war to occupy Gaza and the Sinai Peninsula. Ben-Gurion wanted to annex Gaza but did not want to bring 300,000 Arabs, 215,000 of whom were Palestinian refugees, into the state of Israel. On Nov. 3, 1956, Israeli armed forces invaded the city of Khan Yunis and summarily executed 275 people, more than half of them Palestinian refugees. Similar atrocities were committed in Rafah on Nov. 12, when Israeli forces invaded a refugee camp and killed at least 111 Palestinians; evidence from some eyewitnesses counted 197 dead and 23 disappeared.

Whether or not these massacres were part of a new ethnic cleansing campaign, this time the Palestinians refused to flee. Zionist dreams of taking Gaza had to wait. The UN — backed by both the Soviet Union and the U.S. — forced Israel to pull out.

A few months before the massacres in Gaza, Raphael Lemkin had helped Muhammad H. El-Farra, chief of the UN Section of the Arab States Delegation Office, with an article accusing French officials of committing genocide against Algerians. Published in 1956, "Algeria and the United Nations" is a 56-page indictment detailing atrocities, torture, psychological warfare, and cultural erasure. The evidence compiled led El-Farra to conclude that under French colonial rule the "conditions of life have been deliberately inflicted on the Arab populations to bring about their destruction." In a short piece in *Africa Today*, he summarized the case against France and described the situation on the ground: "Entire villages are shelled, bombed, or burned; acts of genocide are committed against the inhabitants of towns and villages; an indiscriminate campaign of extermination is now taking place; civilians are machine gunned daily by ground forces; summary executions of patriots falling into the hands of French soldiers are likewise carried out. ... These are acts of genocide committed against people whose only crime is their love for liberty and their desire to preserve their own culture." El-Farra was writing not simply as a UN official but as a Palestinian born in Khan Yunis. He grew up in Jaffa, was active in various Arab youth organizations, and left in December 1947 to attend college in the U.S. just as the Nakba unfolded. He recalled fleeing Jaffa under Israeli gunfire, unsure about the fate of his family. He managed to escape the worst of the fighting, but his family's property was confiscated and his brothers dispersed. He could not return right away, and it haunted him. In 1952, while pursuing a law degree from the University of Pennsylvania, he took a research job at the UN information department and worked his way into the Syrian and then Jordanian diplomatic corps.

El-Farra regarded Israel's war and occupation of Palestine as an ongoing genocide that began in 1948, and he devoted the rest of his life trying to stop it. In his 1987 memoir, he asked why Israelis "kill in cold blood" innocent civilians, women, farmers, schoolchildren, and the like. His answer: "It is because they feel that only through the complete destruction of the people of Palestine can they have safety and security in the beloved Palestinian homeland." El-Farra believed the UN was a critical, if flawed, vehicle to stop genocide and possibly bring peace. But it wasn't the only vehicle, he pointed out: "Israel has thus left the Palestinians no other choice but to resist. What else is left for a man who lost everything? Is he to surrender his values and heritage? Should he and his accept being a people without a country, without a future? This would mean their complete destruction, and this is why they have resisted occupation."

The "complete destruction" of a people is the consequence if genocide is not stopped. And there are genocides happening all around us. In Sudan, the indiscriminate killing, torture, rape, and brutality conducted by the Rapid Support Forces constitute an imminent threat of genocide, on a scale that should compel the UN to use all of the powers at its disposal to stop it. Our chants of "Cease-fire now" should ring in every conflict zone, and the lessons of Palestine, South Africa, Namibia, Vietnam, Algeria, Rwanda, Burundi, Congo, India, the former Yugoslavia, and others ought to be remembered: colonialism and its rapacious destruction of the world through dispossession, extraction, racial ordering, war, and partition is what got us here.

*First published in *Hammer & Hope*.

Addendum II

...And How Are the Children?
Paul Hill, Jr.

The Masai of East Africa greet each other with "Casserian Engeri." It means, "And how are the children?" They do not ask each other, "How are you?" or "How's your day?" but instead they ask about the next generation. The Masai believe monitoring the well-being of their children is the best way to determine their society's future health and prosperity.

In the twenty-first century's third decade, what is the global response to the question, "And how are the children?" The children are not well!

The horrific armed conflict in Gaza speaks to a geographically broader and chronic political, moral, and humanitarian crisis. Children are coming under attack in conflicts across the world. This is a moral crisis of the age: We must never accept this as the "new normal." The global atrocities of violence and murder of children and women are unacceptable. Children should never experience harm at the hands of adults. It is especially heinous when the harm occurs as "collateral damage" of adults not being able to find solutions to disagreements other than through senseless violence.

It has been more than 35 years since the adoption of the Convention on the Rights of the Child and more than 70 years since the four Geneva Conventions, the international bedrock to protect civilians in war. It is the time to say, "Enough! Stop attacks on children and women."

The Convention on the Rights of the Child was adopted by the United Nations General Assembly by its resolution 44/25 of November 20, 1989. This was the end of a process that had begun with the preparations for the 1979 International Year of the Child. That year, discussions started on a draft convention submitted by the government of Poland.

Children had been discussed before by the international community. Declarations on the child's rights had been adopted by the League of Nations (1924) and the United States (1959). Also, specific provisions concerning children had been incorporated in several human rights and humanitarian law treaties. Nevertheless, some states argued that there was a need for a comprehensive statement on children's rights that would be binding under international law.

The unanimous adoption of the Convention by the general assembly paved the way for the next stage: state ratifications and setting up a monitoring committee, the Committee on the Rights of the Child. Within less than a year, by September 9, 1990, 20 states had legally endorsed the Convention, which entered into force.

In the same month, the World Summit for Children was held in New York on the initiative of UNICEF and States (Canada, Egypt, Mali, Mexico, Pakistan, and Sweden). The Summit encouraged all States to ratify the Convention. By the end of 1990, 57 had done so, thereby becoming state parties. In 1993, the World Conference on Human Rights held in Vienna declared that the goal was universal ratification by the end of 1995. By December 31, 2015, 196 countries had ratified or acceded to the Convention. All United Nations member states, except the United States of America, have ratified the Convention. The United States argues that ratifying the Convention on the Rights of the Child would limit US sovereignty or cause unlimited interference in family life.

While the United States of America foolishly argues against the ratification of the Convention on the Rights of the Child around the world, attacks on children and family life continue unabated. The number of countries experiencing violent conflict is the highest it has been in 30 years. The result is that more than 30 million children have been displaced by conflict. Many of them are being enslaved, trafficked, abused, and exploited. Many more are living in limbo, without official immigration status or access to education and health care. From Gaza to Ukraine, Afghanistan to Mali, to South Sudan, the Democratic Republic of the Congo, Yemen, Ethiopia, and beyond, warring parties are flouting one of the basic rules of war: "the protection of children." (http://www.worldvison.ca/stories/child-protection/how-armed-conflict-impactschildren#)

The children are not well because of an adult problem, particularly adult males. They are not well because of part-capitalistic values and structures. Patriarchy perpetuates gender-based violence and discrimination, exposing children, especially girls, to various forms of harm. Patriarchal structures and societies are driven by power, control, greed, and privilege. Children and women are expendable. When race, class, gender, ethnicity, religion, economics, and politics are included, the results are toxic and genocidal. Overall, these systems intersect and compound each other, contributing to the vulnerability of children and women in conflict zones globally.

Using this framework, it is essential to understand that what "imperialist white-supremacist capitalist patriarchal society" considers "normal" are tools of oppression. We see how essential items and human needs such as housing, food, electricity, and water are commodified, exploited, and weaponized. Other human needs are also exploited. We must see the need for human connection, equality, and equity, and see as more common and frequent our resistance, as people that occupy spaceship Earth, to violence. We must remove interlocking financial interests in repressive security policies, taking away the profit motive from arms manufacturers, consulting firms, and profit prison industries that benefit from the repression and incarceration of people. We must focus on equitable, non-violent, caring versions of peoplehood. In addition to countering violence, we must build systems that create and measure public goods, public welfare, and social equity.

Addressing the complex issues surrounding conflict and violence and their impact on children requires a multifaceted approach. Some key solutions include:

1. Conflict Prevention—Honestly, resolving conflict and violence requires an understanding of patriarchy and capitalism. Addressing root causes such as inequality, injustice, and marginalization can help prevent conflicts from escalating. Diplomacy, meditation, and peacebuilding efforts are also essential for resolving conflicts peacefully.

2. Protection and Humanitarian Aid—Prioritizing the protection of children in conflict zones through measures such as safe zones, humanitarian corridors, and access to essential services such as food, shelter, healthcare, and education can mitigate harm.

3. Legal Frameworks—Strengthening legal frameworks at national and international levels to protect children in armed conflict, including adherence to international humanitarian law and prosecution of perpetrators of child rights violations.

4. Disarmament and Demobilization—Disarmament, demobilization, and reintegration (DDR) programs aimed at removing children from armed groups, providing them with support and rehabilitation, and reintegrating them into society are crucial for breaking the cycle of violence.

5. Education and Psychosocial Support—Ensuring access to quality education and psychosocial support services for children affected by conflict can mitigate the long-term impacts of trauma and displacement, providing them with

stability and opportunities for growth.

6. Empowering Communities—Empowering communities, in-cluding women and marginal groups, to participate in decision-making processes, promote social cohesion, and address the underlying drivers of conflict can contribute to sustainable peace and stability.

7. Addressing Structural Inequalities—Tackling underlying structural inequalities such as economic disparities, discrimination, and exclusion can help address causes of conflict and create more inclusive societies.

8. Promoting Gender Equality—Promoting gender equality and addressing patriarchal norms and practices that perpetuate violence against women and children are essential and fundamental for creating safer environments for all.

Citizens everywhere can begin by not averting their gaze from children's suffering because it seems too distant or the politics of conflict too complex. We must insist to national and international leaders that protecting children during armed conflict is the cornerstone of our shared humanity.

We must demand leadership which is prepared to act to prevent attacks and violence against children trapped in war zones.

Governments and warring parties where conflicts rage must act to fulfill their obligations to protect ALL children and enable access to specialized response services for children affected by violence.

Communities in conflict-affected areas must be supported to create protective environments for girls and boys.

Governments who support or who have influence over warring parties must use all their influence to insist that ALL children are protected according to the requirements of international law.

International peace and security institutions such as the United Nations Security Council and regional organizations can do more to prioritize the safety and well-being of children.

The international community can do more to support programs which work to protect children from violence, abuse, and exploitation, and deliver the services needed to help children come through conflict with hope for a better future.

By protecting children from attacks in armed conflict, we keep hope alive; we begin to prepare children to shape peaceful futures for themselves and their countries. Acting together, we can turn back this deadly 'new normal' of attacks against children and women and preserve humanity.

Overall, a comprehensive approach that addresses the immediate needs of children in conflict zones and the underlying driver of conflict is necessary to ensure their protection and well-being. Collaboration between governments, international organizations, and local communities is essential for effective implementation of these solutions. Moving forward as people, countries, and nations, we need economic and political systems that value and prioritize All children. Until we as leaders and decision-makers at all system levels can ask and answer the question, "And how are the children?" with a response, "The children are well," we are doomed!

References

Allan, Ellie. "Capitalism and Patriarchy Are Inseparable." *The Gazelle*, 20, Mar. 2021, www.thegazelle.org/issue/199/capitalism-patriarchy- inseperable

Bak, Whitney, and Emily Neilson Jones. "Understanding Patriarchy Intersectional Insights of Bell Hooks." *The Girl Child, and Her Long Walk to Freedom*, 9 Aug. 2020, girlchildlongwalk.org/ understanding patriarchy-intersectional-insights-of-bell- hooks/

Barker, Gary. "Male Violence or Patriarchal Violence? Global Trends in Men and Violence." *Sexualidad, Salud Y Sociedad (Rio De Janeiro)*, no. 22, Apr. 2016, pp. 316-30, https://doi.org/10.1590/1984- 6487.sess.2016.22.14.a.

Hardoon, Deborah. "Wealth: Having It All and Wanting More." *OXFAM International*, 19 Jan. 2015, www.oxfam.org/en/research/wealth having-it-all-and-wanting-more

Kanuha, Val Kalei. "Colonization and Violence against Women." *Asian Pacific Institute on Gender-Based Violence*, 2002, www.api-gbv. org resources/colonization-violence-against-women/

Ostby, Gudrun, et al. "Children Affected by Armed Conflict (1990-2022)." *Relief Web*, 14 Dec. 2023, reliefweb.int/report/world/children- affected-armed-conflict-1990-2022

Vision, World. "How Armed Conflict Impacts Children." World Vision, 15 Aug. 2023, www.worldvision.ca/stories/child-protection/how- armed-conflict-impacts-children

Addendum III

Might Say, 10/14/2023*

Keith Gilyard

Unless it's going to be all war all the time in the land of old Palestine, a political solution must be sought. That a viable one to balance peacefully the existence of the state of Israel with justice for five million people in an apportioned Palestine---three million in the West Bank and two million in Gaza---has not been found in seventy-five years speaks to the difficulty of the task. The reasons for failure number several historical, political, economic, and religious ones, of course. Maybe a rhetoric cannot be found to work through all that productively. But it's always worth trying to get the language right. Such a task seems especially urgent to me when I watch dominant media coverage of unfolding events and responses on campuses such as Harvard and UCLA. I make three quick points in this regard.

First, life must mean life. The horror of the October 7th attacks by Hamas is undeniable. Women, men, and children, hundreds of children, mowed down mercilessly. Understandably, somebody is going to want to get their lick back and will do it. This is what Netanyahu is saying to Blinken when he shows him pictures of the atrocities. Blinken, upping the ante on the old saying that a picture is worth a thousand words, responds that these pictures are worth millions of words. How many millions of words, though, are pictures of dead children in Gaza worth? Are the children's lives equivalent? Is Blinken differentiating, creating a variable scale of life, when he declares that the United States will always stand with Israel? Or as the celebrated Palestinian-American poet Naomi Shihab Nye---great poets are always useful---writes in "A Palestinian Might Say": "Where before you mingled freely / appreciated people who weren't / just like you / divisions grow stronger / That's what 'chosen' and 'unchosen' will do." In other words, that's what the rhetoric of chosen and unchosen will do. So life must mean life. None being the unchosen, unreal life against a really real chosen one.

Second, call an imperialist occupation what it is. We do it regarding Crimea and Donetsk, and the United States government has spent over forty billion dollars for Ukrainians to resist. Now there are all kinds of special-interest reasons for not calling the Israeli government's imperialist occupation of Palestine the Israeli government's imperialist occupation of Palestine. But refusing truth won't change truth---and certainly isn't a fruitful way to talk about truth. I wonder if or when they'll include statements of land acknowledgment on syllabi in Israeli colleges and universities the way they do in the U.S. with respect to Native Americans.

Speaking of universities and the demonstrations at UCLA and Harvard brings me to my third language point, that is, the need to recognize anti-Zionism and anti-Semitism as false equivalents. To express opposition to the Zionist project espoused by the likes of Theodor Herzl, David Ben-Gurion, on down is to reject a policy proposal and mission of conquest. That is not anti-Semitism if such is taken to mean prejudice against or hatred of Jews as Jews. This point is missed by students waving the flag of Israel near UCLA as a counterstatement to critics of the Israeli government and by the doxxers driving around Harvard Square to out students who belong to the thirty student groups that signed a statement asserting that the Israeli government was responsible for the unfolding violence. Nuance and detail are needed but not always welcome on this topic. Ask Jimmy Carter about the reception of his book *Palestine: Peace Not Apartheid*, including the resignation of fourteen people from the Carter Center community board.

I ponder this when I listen and imagine, thinking of Naomi Shihab Nye's poem again, what various people might say.

*First published in *The Language Lane*.

Contributors

Zahra Ali is Associate Professor of Sociology at Rutgers University-Newark. Her work explores (racial) capitalism, (post)coloniality, decolonial theory, and transnational feminisms as well as critical knowledge making and epistemologies with a focus on Iraq, the Middle East, and Muslim communities. She is the author of *Women and Gender in Iraq* published by Cambridge University Press, and co-editor of *Decolonial Pluriversalism* published by Rowman & Littlefield.

Molefi Kete Asante is a philosopher, poet, and activist intellectual who lives in Philadelphia. He is the author of *Africa's Gifts of the Spirit.*

J. Raya Bell is a professor of environmental philosophy and critical race theory who is committed to transdisciplinary scholarship reflecting their ongoing understanding of issues around racial, gender, environmental, food, and class justice. They are sought after for research, teaching, public speaking, and lectures across the subjects of traditional ecological knowledge, women's reproductive health, and sustainable food systems.

Herb Boyd-- On three trips to the holy land, the first with Stokely Carmichael (Kwame Ture), I learned firsthand about some of the legends and conflicts there that seem to be without end. Now the images of a devastated Gaza and the humanitarian crisis, particularly the wretched conditions of the children, compel me to join my comrades in registering our complaint about the terrible injustice.

Jason Cohen is a Marxist-Leninist activist active in the Workers World Party and Friends of Swazi Freedom. Jason recently obtained a master's in history from the City College of New York. He is a Puerto Rican Jew from New York City.

T. Elon Dancy II is Executive Director, Center for Urban Education, and Helen S. Faison Endowed Chair in Urban Education at the University of Pittsburgh.

Lara Friedman is the president of the Foundation for Middle East Peace (FMEP). A leading authority on the Middle East and U.S. foreign policy in the region, Lara is a former officer in the U.S. Foreign Service, with diplomatic postings in Jerusalem, Washington, Tunis, and Beirut. She also served previously as Director of Policy and Government Relations at Americans for Peace Now.

Brian Gilmore, a native of Washington, DC, is a poet, public interest lawyer, and senior lecturer in the Law and Society Program at the University of Maryland-College Park. He has authored four collections of poetry, including *elvis presley is alive and well and living in harlem* and *come see about me marvin*.

Keith Gilyard is Edwin Erle Sparks Professor of English and African American studies at Penn State. He is author or editor of thirty books, including *Discourse in Black* and *The Promise of Language*. He has received two American Book Awards.

Dr. Edmund W. Gordon is John M. Musser Professor of Psychology Emeritus, Yale University; Richard March Hoe Professor of Psychology and Education Emeritus, Teachers College, Columbia University; and the founding director of the Institute for Urban and Minority Education (IUME) at Teachers College, Columbia University. After Third World Press recently published Dr. Gordon's three volume autobiography, *Pedagogical Imagination: A Conceptual Memoir Volume I, II, & III*, we were happy to have been a part of the celebration of his recent 103rd birthday.

Heba Gowayed is Associate Professor of Sociology at CUNY Hunter College and The Graduate Center. Her work centers the lives of people who migrate across borders and the unequal and often violent institutions they face. She is author of *Refuge*, published with Princeton University Press, and is working on her second project, *The Cost of Borders*, in which she argues that borders, rather than being moral markers of sovereign land, are better understood as a series of expensive, and often deadly, transactions.

Gabriel I. Green is Assistant Professor of African American Literature at Xavier University of Louisiana. His prize-winning poetry chapbook, *The Magical Negro Reveals His Secret*, was published by C&R Press in 2019.

Talib Kweli Greene is one of the world's most talented, accomplished, and socially conscious hip-hop artists. His book, *Vibrate Higher: A Rap Story*, is a first-hand account of hip hop as a political force. Over the last twenty-four years, Kweli has produced eight solo albums, collaborated on nine albums, performed nationally and internationally, and created podcasts.

Tracie D. Hall, librarian and public scholar, was recently named Distinguished Practitioner in Residence at the University of Washington Information School and is former executive director of the American Library Association, the first Black woman to hold that title in the organization's nearly 150 years. Focused on early and adult literacy, broadband access, and library and literacy services for the incarcerated, Hall's work in library and arts administration has been recognized with the National Book Foundation Lifetime Achievement Award, recognition on the TIME Magazine list of the 100 Most Influential People of 2023, and the 2023 Medal for Freedom of Speech and Free Expression from the Roosevelt Institute.

Rev. Dr. Marshall Elijah Hatch, Sr. serves as Senior Pastor at New Mount Pilgrim Missionary Baptist Church of Chicago; as Professor of Ministry at Northern Seminary, where he is the Inaugural Director of the Center for Black Church Studies; and on the Board Trustees of Baptist Theological Union, University of Chicago Divinity School.

Marc Lamont Hill, a social justice activist and organizer since his days as a youth in Philadelphia, is one of the leading intellectual voices in the country. He has worked in solidarity with human rights movements around the world. Currently a Presidential Professor of Anthropology and Urban Education at the City University of New York Graduate Center, his current research and writing explore the relationships among race, culture, politics, and education in the United States and the Middle East. His books include *Beats, Rhymes, and Classroom Life: Hip-Hop Pedagogy and the Possibilities of Identity; The Classroom and The Cell: Conversations on Black Life in America; Nobody: Casualties of America's War on the Vulnerable, from Ferguson to Flint and Beyond; We Still Here: Pandemic, Policing, Protest, and Possibility;* and *Except For Palestine: The Limits of Progressive Politics.*

Paul Hill, Jr., MSW, LISW, is a noted author, social worker, researcher, and practitioner of rites of passage (ROP). For over thirty years, he served as head of a multi-service community organization, providing youth, adults, and elders with acclaimed programming in Cleveland, Ohio. Hill is publisher of the peer-reviewed, semi-annual, *Black Child Journal.* He has been a devoted husband to Marquita McAllister Hill for fifty-five years, is a proud father of seven children, grandfather of ten, and has been a valued mentor to countless youth, students, community leaders, and others throughout his life.

Ezra Hyland teaches at the University of Minnesota, and his community service includes being a local host of the African American Read-In and serving as Board Chair of the Harvest Best Academy and Wakanda Virtual Academy, Afrocentric schools whose mission is to instruct, empower, enable, and guide children to achieve superior academic, social, and moral development.

Marilyn Kallet, Professor Emerita at the University of Tennessee, is a former Knoxville Poet Laureate and has also published numerous poetry volumes, including *Packing Light, How Our Bodies Learned,* and *Even When We Sleep.*

Dr. Maulana Karenga Dr. Maulana Karenga is a professor and chair of the Department of Africana Studies, California State University, Long Beach. An activist-scholar of national and international recognition, he is executive director of the African American Cultural Center (Us) and the National Association of Kawaida Organizations. Dr. Karenga is the creator of the pan-African cultural holiday *Kwanzaa* and the *Nguzo Saba*, and author of numerous scholarly articles and books, including *Maat, The Moral Ideal in Ancient Egypt.*

Robin D. G. Kelley is Gary B. Nash Professor of American History at UCLA. His essays have appeared in a wide variety of professional journals as well as general publications, including the *Journal of American History, American Historical Review, The Nation, New York Times, The Black Scholar, Journal of Palestine Studies,* and *Boston Review,* for which he also serves as Contributing Editor. His numerous authored and edited books include the eleven-volume *Young Oxford History of African Americans* (with Earl Lewis); *Freedom Dreams: The Black Radical Imagination;* and *Africa Speaks, America Answers: Modern Jazz in Revolutionary Times.*

Aneb Kgositsile (also known as Gloria House, PhD) is an educator, essayist, poet, and freedom worker. She lives in Detroit, where she is an activist in the African American liberation movement.

Haki R. Madhubuti, University Distinguished Professor Emeritus, Chicago State University, is a best-selling poet, author, and educator. Widely regarded as one of the architects of the Black Arts Movement (BAM), he is the founder and publisher of Chicago's Third World Press. In 2015, the publishing house expanded its mission as Third World Press Foundation. Madhubuti is also a co-founder of both the Institute of Positive Education and the Betty Shabazz International Charter Schools, an African-centered institution, which operates three schools in Chicago. Madhubuti has authored or edited dozens of books, including his most recent, *Taught by Women: Poems as Resistance Language.* He has produced four albums/CDs with music, and his poetry and essays have been included in more than one hundred anthologies.

Dr. Julianne Malveaux is an economist, author, and educator. She is President Emerita of Bennett College in Greensboro, North Carolina, and Inaugural Dean (2021-2023) of the College of Ethnic Studies at California State University at Los Angeles. Currently, she is an independent scholar based in Washington, DC, writing a book about lynching culture and the wealth gap. The second edition of her book, *Surviving and Thriving: 365 Facts in Black Economic History,* is available from www.speakloudly.com.

Tony Medina, born in the South Bronx and raised in the Throgs Neck Housing Projects, is a multi-genre author/editor of twenty-five award-winning books for adults and young people, the most recent of which are *Rock the Bells: For Hip Hop @ 50*, (hybrid), *Che Che Colé* (fiction); *Death, With Occasional Smiling* (poetry); *Thirteen Ways of Looking at a Black Boy* (children's); *I Am Alfonso* Jones (graphic novel); and *Resisting Arrest: Poems to Stretch the Sky* (anthology). The first Professor of Creative Writing at Howard University, Medina holds a master's and PhD from Binghamton University, SUNY.

Mursalata Muhammad is a professor of English at Grand Rapids Community College in Michigan. Dr. Muhammad's poetry has appeared in anthologies and online publications. She is an ally for children, lifelong learner, and public servant.

Michael Simanga is a multi-discipline activist artist, writer, producer, and educator. He teaches Africana Studies at Morehouse College and has written and edited several books, including *Amiri Baraka and the Congress of African People; In the Shadow of the Son: A Novel;* and *No One Can Be at Peace Unless They Have Freedom*. His poetry and essays have been published in several anthologies on Black life, politics, and art.

Rahiel Tesfamariam, known as a leading generational voice, is an award-winning activist, journalist, theologian, and international speaker with decades of impactful community organizing and media experience. A former *Washington Post* columnist, she is the founder of *Urban Cusp*, a cutting-edge online community. Rahiel's debut book, *Imagine Freedom: Transforming Pain into Political and Spiritual Power*, is available wherever books are sold.

Jonathan Tilove worked forty-five years as a reporter for newspapers in Springfield, Massachusetts; New Orleans; and Austin. For twenty of those years, he served as a national reporter for Newhouse Newspapers, based in Washington, DC, where he wrote about race. He is the author, with photographer Michael Falco, of *Along Martin Luther King: Travels on Black America's Main Street*, published in 2003 by Random House and reissued in paperback in 2024 by Third World Press, for which he is writing a memoir.

Sabina Vaught is an educator and scholar. She currently works as a professor at the University of Pittsburgh.

Alice Walker is an American novelist, short story writer, poet, and social activist. In 1982, she became the first African American woman to win the Pulitzer Prize for Fiction, which she was awarded for her novel *The Color Purple*. Walker has published more than thirty books of fiction, nonfiction, and poetry.

Rabbi Alissa Wise is the lead organizer of Rabbis for Ceasefire, which she founded in October 2023. She is co-author with Rebecca Vilkomerson of *Solidarity Is the Political Version of Love: Lessons from Jewish Anti-Zionist Organizing.*

Christopher M. Wright is a PhD candidate and graduate research and teaching associate in the University of Pittsburgh Center for Urban Education.

Dave Zirin is sports editor of the *Nation.* He is the author of eleven books on the politics of sports, including his latest, *The Kaepernick Effect.*

Third World Press Foundation anticipates publishing a volume to increase awareness about the crisis that has been intensifying over the past eighteen months in Sudan. More than 5 million people have been displaced by military conflict, and more than 7 million people, *one-third of whom are children,* now suffer from malnutrition and lack access to clean water and essential medical services. Queries are welcome from prospective editors and writers.